Shirley Botsford's
Daddy's Ties

A Project & Keepsake Book

Chilton Book Company
One Chilton Way
Radnor, Pennsylvania

Published in Radnor. Pennsylvania by Chilton Book Company

Project designs and directions by Shirley Botsford
Editorial direction by Robbie Fanning and Kathy Conover
Computer graphics by Merritt Graphics
Illustrations by Roger Craig Merritt
Photography by Roger Craig Merritt
Bowjolais Photo on page 92-Fairfield Processing Corp.
Printed by R.R. Donnelley & Sons Company
Cover photograph projects: Bow Tie Beauty Wall Hanging, Log Cabin Pillow On Point, Grandma's Fan
Toss Pillow, Tie-ler The Teddy, Crazy Chunk Framed, Souvenir Tie Ball
Leather chair from Hudson Valley Office Supply

First Printing
Manufactured in the United States of America

Library of Congress Cataloging-in-Publication Data

Botsford, Shirley J
    Daddy's Ties
    Shirley Botsford's Daddy's Ties : a project and keepsake book.
    p. cm.
    Includes index.
    ISBN 0-8019-8521-8
    1. Patchwork--Patterns.   2. Neckties.   3.Household linens.
4. Soft toys.   Title; I. Title II. Title; Daddy's Ties.
TT835 . B834   1994
746 . 46--dc20   94-21722
                                                          CIP

2 3 4 5 6 7 8 9 0 3 2 1 0 9 8 7 6 5

DEDICATION

This book is dedicated to all the women who sew. Especially the ones who save things and recycle fabrics. And, especially those who use needlework as a means of expression and creativity. It is dedicated to anyone who has ever taken apart a garment or something old and then made something new from it. I have a class that I just love to teach, called "New From Old ." For this class, I ask everyone to bring a fabric item that they have saved, like an old tablecloth, dresser scarf, a child's dress, or yes, men's ties. It's wonderful to see the different things that everyone brings. But no matter what it is, it's always something that means something to them and has memories attached to it. It seems like the class time just flies by because, while we stitch, each student takes a turn, telling a personal story about the "old" fabric item that they brought. During the class, I show them how to take apart and cut up the old and create something new. Some students find it hard to cut into their pieces, but when the class is over, they're always glad that they shared their stories and made something new from something old. Whatever they make, it's something that will be cherished too and something that will create new memories. And something that they will want to save and perhaps recycle again someday.

Shirley Botsford

ACKNOWLEDGMENTS

I would like to thank everyone who has helped make this book possible.   Especially my father, James Botsford, who taught me that you can always make it better yourself, and my mother, Jean Denzinger Botsford, who taught me how. And, my brother, Gary Botsford, who never wore a tie in his life!

Even though the message in this book is do-it-yourself, one thing that you can't do yourself is a book like this. It takes lots of people with lots of talent and lots of patience to make it happen. I'd like to thank those wonderful, talented, patient friends in print so, perhaps, I can get them to help me on my next book, too.

Roger Craig Merritt	Virginia Avery	Ann Boyce-Kline
Pam Hoffman	Donna Wilder	Marinda Stewart
Janet Jappen	Janice Peterson Johnson	Shirley Fowlkes

I am especially grateful for the help and encouragement of my new friends at Chilton who made it possible to get this book published: Susan Clarey, Kathy Conover, Mike Campell, Tony Jacobson, Nancy Ellis, Janine La Borne, Carla Williams, Karen Miltko

Also, deserving of thanks are all the friends who have donated ties and fabrics and support for this book. A special thank you goes to Rosebar Fabrics for the unlimited supply of wonderful iridescent taffetas. When I started writing this book, I did a great deal of hanging out at thrift shops and the Salvation Army. looking for ties. It became impossible to get enough ties to make all the projects and my friends generously responded with their ties.

Pat Eagen
Margaret Peters
Dave Pike for his father Samuel Pike
Oscar Gamble - W.O. Gamble, Paducah, KY
Charlene Turnbough - Love My Fabrics
Melissa and Peter Lourie for the leftover scraps from their wonderful burgundy velvet sofa.
The Men of Grace Lutheran Church - Allentown, PA
Corinne Dickson for her husband Roy
Elaine Whalen-Pedersen
Mary and Ken Lynn

Marguerite M. Merritt	Countess Mara	Violet Hoffman
Norman A. Merritt	Robbie Fanning	William Roberts
Jim Crowley	Marilyn & Ed Callaway	William Gaul
Rita & Len Donchez	Jean & Jim Botsford	Paul Hendricks
Henry Steve Stevenson	Priscilla Miller	Richard C. Klick
Peter Jurutka	Asher Pavel	Cynthia Liebler
Joan & Jerry Silverberg	Mark Fulling	Dr. William Liebler

A personal word of thanks to my sewing and quilting friends for their enthusiastic support ...and their ties!

Jaye Vaughn	Kathi Schmitter	Elizabeth Conrad
Kay Erenzo	Joyce Moshier	Shirley Wersebe
Rene Horvath	Elena McHerron	Rosalie Fagan

CONTENTS

FOREWORD

No one out-shines Shirley Botsford when it comes to creativity. Her rare instinctive ability enables her to predict trends and to creatively develop patterns for crafts and wearables that follow these trends. The success of Shirley's patterns is well known throughout the craft industry and for this reason, companies often consult with her on new craft projects and products.

I can't remember when I first met Shirley, but I know it was around 1981 when the designers for the 1982 Fairfield Fashion Show were being selected. Several people had suggested Shirley as a possible designer, and I had seen many of her designs featured in crafts magazines. I felt, at the time, that Shirley would add a new dimension to the show and I was not disappointed! Shirley has dazzled the audiences for years with spectacular one-of-a-kind extravaganzas, such as the Braided Bride, Victorian Star and the Blonde Bombshell. But, of all the garments she has made, none has moved me as much as Daddy's Ties, one that she created for RADIANT STAR, the 1984 Fairfield Fashion Show.

Shirley's father passed away just before the time she was deliberating over what to make for the fashion show. She became inspired by his many ties while they were cleaning out his closet and preparing to send them to the Salvation Army. She just couldn't bear to see this happen, she kept thinking of the many memories those wonderful ties evoked and she knew she had to pay special tribute to her father by utilizing his ties. Thus, her garment entitled Daddy's Ties was created!

Shirley has developed additional projects and patterns using ties. She shares these exciting new ideas with you in DADDY'S TIES and makes it possible for you to create your own keepsakes. I know you will be as impressed as I am with the many innovative uses she has uncovered for ties. So, clean out your partner's closet, check out the Salvation Army and you too can create with your own tie collection. Keep in mind, no tie is too ugly. Let your imagination go and have fun with these creative ideas from Shirley Botsford!

Donna Wilder

INTRODUCTION

Ifeel honored that Shirley has asked me to write this introduction. This book is a testimony to her awesome talent. Daddy's Ties isn't just your run of the mill craft book - it's a composite of great ideas carried out in minute detail. The designs and projects are stunning, and there's something here for everyone - the quilter, the fashion maven, the home dec addict and all the others - those who want to make everything and those who want to make a single gift or a stocking stuffer. Shirley's instructions are clear and concise, and heaven knows they should be, for she's an old hand at this.

Shirley is an established New York designer of almost twenty years, and her name is a byword at Simplicity, Woman's Day, Family Circle and Good Housekeeping. She's designed everything from fabric lines for Wamsutta and Springs to whole collections of crafts tools and has written numerous books on sewing, quilting and crafting.

Her background is substantial. After completing the course at Traphagen School of Fashion in New York, she attended and graduated from the Moore College of Art in Philadelphia, majoring in both textile design and art education. After working a short while in both Philly and New York, she decided to try it on her own and go into business for herself. As they say in the best cliche circles, the rest is history.

I knew her name long before I knew her, then she catapulted into my life with her entry "Daddy's Ties" in the Fairfield Fashion Show a few years back. For you enlightened readers, the original "Daddy's Ties" outfit was an ankle length gown with fitted bodice, full circular skirt and a waist-length vest. Both gown and vest were made of ties - her father's; each tie in the gown separated by a strip of black lace, and the vest composed of bowties. The whole effect was a symphony of glowing rich pattern and color; it was also a loving tribute to her father's memory, and it stopped the show. As you probably know, the Fairfield show travels for a year, and at each performance, the acclaim was the same, tumultuous. If you want to know how I felt about it, I just couldn't believe it. Not only was "Daddy's Ties" a major triumph of design, but it was exquisitely engineered, and on top of that, Shirley turned out to be a bright and lovely blonde, sharing, caring, funny, gifted, creative, perceptive ...well, you get the idea.

This book is, of course, a result of that first creation. It didn't take Shirley long to realize what a goldmine there was in ties, in the colors and patterns and the rich, top quality silk. She proved her point by making all the samples in the book. The photography is excellent and she doesn't just show you a picture of something and tell you to make it out of ties: she takes you through each step, holding your hand all the way. She tells you how to take the ties apart, wash out all the gravy and catsup stains, and prepare them for a heady trip of recycling. You and your home can both be well dressed by following Shirley's leads. I can see a sofa in your home piled high with pillows - old quilt patterns transformed. I can see your walls hung with stunning examples of still other quilt patterns - they never had it so good! I can see you too, in a wonderful jacket of tie silks, collecting compliments in your wake, and I even see you cuddling that tie silk teddy bear. Who wouldn't?

Well, the path ahead is clear. Shirley has laid out a tie feast for all of us. There's no such thing as sampling. You'll overeat and love every bite. You'll also be out there rummaging around at tag and garage sales, at the Salvation Army and Goodwill bins, looking for ties and hoping Shirley didn't get there first. You'll also be quietly assessing the ties owned by the men in your life and wondering if you snitched one or two if it would be noticed. You must encourage your men to add to their tie collections, and every now and then give them one to show that you mean business. Your standards of friendship may change; from now on, you may cultivate new men friends not by their Wall Street reputations but by what they wear around their necks. There's hope for married women, too. The Kansas City Star reported not long ago that every year, the fathers in the U.S. get 12,600 miles of ties for Father's Day. So far the mileage has not been reported for Christmas or birthdays.

Enough is enough. This book is hot stuff, so get going and tie one on....

Virginia Avery

CHAPTER 1

New From Old

How I Got Interested in Ties

A few months after my dad died, the day came to clear out his closets. The presence of his clothes had become a concern for everyone in the family. On the spur of the moment, we all decided to work together and make shuttle runs to the nearest clothes donation box. After a few trips with the trunk full of plastic garbage bags, it was almost done. I was loading the car with the last few things and discovered a half-dozen brown paper grocery bags lined up along one wall in the garage. They were full of Daddy's ties. For some compelling reason I just couldn't let them go. I peeked into one bag and spotted a few really awful ones that I remembered personally selecting for my Dad's birthday. What a sport, he always made me think that these were his favorites. Well, that settles it, these were going with me! If Dad saved them all these years, then I would too.

The bags of ties sat in the corner of my studio for almost a year. Every once in a while I'd dump one of them out and line all the ties up on the cutting table and just enjoy looking at them. Then, one day a letter arrived from Donna Wilder at Fairfield Processing inviting me to create a garment for the annual designer fashion show, Now I knew why I saved all those ties. I spent the next few months working on the design for the dress,...and remembering my wonderful Dad. Daddy would have loved it and I named the dress "Daddy's Ties."

My Tie Diary

Whenever possible, I've included a place for you to record your own individual personal tie history. 'My Tie Diary' spaces are special places for you to include your own swatches, photos and information about the projects you plan to make. I was always told that you should never write in a book, but you have my permission to just go ahead and write directly in this book. Feel free to add comments, sketches and ideas wherever you like. Please make this book your very own keepsake that will stay in the family as a record of all the things that you made with ties.

Collecting Old Ties

The best route is to collect ties from relatives. And get them to ask their relatives, and friends, and neighbors. You probably won't have to pay for these and you know where they came from. I think it's really fun to make a project from someone's own ties and then give it back to them in the form of a wonderful recycled gift. Keep this in

mind when you select a tie as a gift. It may come back to you later. I know that I will never choose a tie for someone in the same way again.

Keep in mind that ties, like almost everything else, are collectibles. Watch for very old or unusual ones. If you think you might have something really special on your hands, consult a vintage clothing collector or dealer to find out if it is really valuable before you cut it up. Hollywood Reporter columnist, George Christy is a tie connoisseur and collector and has a magnificent collection of ties made from the '20's to the '50's. He says, "...if you have a tie that was made before 1950, in mint condition, don't touch it before you do a bit of research. Occasionally I find one in it's original box that has never been worn. Some of these ties have become quite valuable to tie collectors over the last few years and cutting them up would be unthinkable. Even if they turn out not to be worth a lot of money, they make great conversation pieces and wearing them has definitely compensated for the small fortune that I have spent in dry cleaning."

Where to Find Ties

There are always the obvious places to start looking - thrift shops, consignment shops, bazaars, used clothing stores and don't forget the closets of all your men friends. It seems like most men have lots more ties than they will ever need and with a little encouragement, will probably part with a few that they're not too fond of. Let the word get out that you're looking and you'll be surprised how many responses you get. After announcing her need for ties at church one day, one of my students told me that she would find a bag of ties placed by her mailbox almost every day for several weeks. Sometimes, just knowing that there's a good use for their ties will motivate people to sort through them and let some of them go.

My Tie Diary

My name:

How many ties I have:

Who they belonged to:

How I got them:

What I plan to make:

The date I started:

Who will receive my project:

Organizations and churches that take donations of old clothing are the best place to seriously search for ties. They receive them frequently so, unless I've already been there, you'll probably have lots to choose from. Be sure to let the person in charge know what you're going to make with them. Sometimes, if they know how many you're looking for, you might be able to make a good deal. Once I almost left this thrift shop because they only had three really terrible ties on display. After explaining why I had such a big appetite for ties, the nice person behind the counter led me to an old refrigerator box absolutely full of great ones that had just come in. The more people that you talk to about your tie projects, the more ties you'll get. If you know of a group that might have some ties, that doesn't have a retail shop, offer to make a donation in exchange for any ties that come in.

At another place where I found lots of ties, they just used them to tie up old mattresses and furniture. They just never thought that anyone would ever have any other use for them. Probably because of me, more and more sewers are looking for ties and I am now actually running into other tie seekers on my regular tie quests. There's lots of competition and some of these beautiful ties are actually worth fighting for. After heading out on one of my tie safaris, I laughed to myself over the potential headlines in the evening paper, "Woman jailed after brawl over old men's ties!" Do keep your tie procurement activities legal!

Try placing a small ad in your local paper. "Old Men's Ties Wanted!" I did this and received some great responses from old men. Later, I revised this to read, "Men's old ties wanted." Now mind you, the age of the tie owners is of no concern, except I have found that the older the tie, the more I seem to like it. So go beg, ask everyone, advertise and just start collecting them. No matter how you come by them, the ties themselves will eventually entice you to make something wonderful. Oh, by the way, you can always send any that you don't use to me.

100% Silk or What?

I'm not much of a silk snob when it comes to tie fabrics. I like them all. Of course, silk is my favorite, but I find that my projects are much more interesting if other fabrics are mixed in with them. You'll come across all varieties of synthetic blends, polyesters in different weaves, wools, crepe's, cotton, linen and unusual knits. It's not necessary for the fabrics to be the same weight, but avoid combining very flimsy ones with the extra heavies in the same project. I have found that tie fabrics are as varied as the designs that are printed on them and the more you mix them up, the more fantastic the results.

Tie Tack-Tics

Knit ties are great for braiding or weaving, but do not piece well. I've used them in my Crazy Chunks with great results, but they're not as versatile as other ties. Three textured knit ties braided together make a wonderful stretchy headband or belt.

Inspect your ties carefully. Look for worn edges and badly faded colors. Watch out for a possibly perforated "tie-tack area"! This part can be badly damaged by having holes punched in it over and over again. If your ties are in really bad shape, try braiding them or weaving them. This is a great way to use them so the worn or torn areas really don't show.

Each tie, depending on it's condition, yields only a narrow strip of fabric. You will need 16 to 20 ties to equal a yard of fabric. Also, it's a good idea to start your project with a few extra on hand.

Remember that if you are working with old ties, you are working with antique fabrics. These can behave unpredictably sometimes and might disappoint you. Old ties have probably been stored in a dark and sometimes damp place. Chances are that no textile conservation methods were used to preserve the fabrics. When you bring them out into the light and expose them to wear, be aware that they will react to how you handle them. I have had a few pieces shred or disintegrate but washing generally weeds out the ones that are going to cause you problems. When storing or using your projects, handle them gently and avoid excess heat, light, moisture, chemicals, etc.

Families of Ties

It's fun to gather together all the ties from one owner to make a project. It fascinates me how one individual's collection of ties always seems to go together. This makes sense because they were probably selected or purchased over the years by the same person, to go with the same suits. They directly reflect the style and color preferences of their wearer. When someone gives me their ties, I try to keep them together in the same project for sentimental reasons, but they often go together better than any combination that I might dream up on my own.

Frequently, when I start a project, the ties that I have to choose from just don't seem to work together as far as color and design. None of them are what I want and some could definitely be classified as "uglies". That's because I'm looking at them as individual ties and not as bits and pieces of my design. Don't hesitate to start just because you hate the ties that you have. This happens in my classes all the time. You know ... my ties aren't as nice as her ties! Well, stop worrying and just start cutting. Something wonderful happens when you combine even the worst ones together. I tested this out by taking all the ties in my studio that I had rejected from other projects and used them together to make a vest. It turned out great and has since become my favorite vest. My students are always surprised and usually delighted at how wonderful all their own tie fabrics blend together no matter how hesitant they were in the beginning. So don't spend any extra time selecting the perfect ties, just get going.

Cheating if You Can't Find any Ties

If you have a few ties, but not enough to make the project you want, just mix them with fabrics that you can buy by the yard. Frequently, the ties that you can find aren't in the colors that you want to use. Experiment mixing ties with all kinds of fabrics. I just love the combination of ties and iridescent taffetas in different colors. They blend beautifully together and the look is much less "busy" than when you use ties exclusively for your project. You can also select the dominant colors that you want for your project by using fabrics and simply accenting them with a small assortment of "gourmet" tie fabrics.

Substitutes for Ties

Lots of people don't exactly relish the idea of working with old ties, especially those of unknown origin. Not to mention the time involved in turning them into useable pieces of fabric. The reason for using old ties

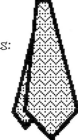

My Tie Diary

Some swatches of my favorite ties:

The source of these ties:

My Tie Diary

Some of my favorite colors:

Swatches of fabric I'd like to use with my ties:

is the antique quality of the fabric and the beautiful patina that they have from being worn. However, you can come pretty close to that look by using some new fabrics. Even though this book is about ties, most of the projects could also be made with your favorite fabrics, even cottons. Ties have provided the inspiration, but you can choose the fabrics that you like to work with. Check out the fancy fabrics at your local fabric shop. Look at the brocades, taffetas, silks, failles, moires, jacquards, linings and evening fabrics. These work great combined with real ties or all by themselves. Get a few 1/4 yard cuts of your favorites and experiment with them. Something I do that always works well is develop a textured, one-color theme. Select an assortment of different fabric types and designs in the same color family. Shiny ones next to stripes, then slubby ones with geometrics, stick in some

lace... anything goes! These easy unexpected combinations create lots of excitement. After you experience success with this, branch out into multi-colored versions of the same idea.

Antique Your Own

Another thing I like to do is simply "distress" new fabrics so they look like old ones. Have you ever seen those terrifying words, DRY CLEAN ONLY, printed on the end of a bolt of wonderful fabric? Well, this just appeals to my rebellious nature and the first thing that I do when I get home is throw it in the washer. This, of course, will damage the fabric... and that's just what I want to do to achieve an "antiqued" look. I've been doing this for years and I almost always know how things will turn out. However, to avoid any surprises, it's a good idea to test this on a small scrap before you plunge yards and yards of expensive fabric into the washer. If you don't like the results, just make yourself a stunning evening outfit, and then definitely dry clean only.

New Tie Fabrics

The best of both worlds is to find new tie fabrics. If this sounds too good to be true, here are a few suggestions. Better menswear shops often receive swatches of tie fabrics from which they do their buying. Some of these shops just throw the swatches away so it couldn't hurt to ask. Many fabric stores that carry odd-lots and close-outs will have a bolt or two of tie fabric stashed

away somewhere. Check the lining section of the store for tie fabric "look-alikes". Some imported oriental silks and high-quality lining fabrics blend well with ties, making it look like you have more ties than you really do.

Tie Scraps by Mail

I recently found out about a great source for scraps from the cutting room floor of a real tie factory that I would like to pass on to you. The Robert Talbott Studio sells wonderful new tie scraps from their factory and will ship them to you. The assortment is based on limited seasonal availability and their factory production at the time of your order. The selection is entirely up to them. But, I'm sure you won't be disappointed with their choices. Ordering information is included in the Source List. ❖

CHAPTER 2

Turning Ties Into Projects

Now that you've got your ties, you need to get them into shape to use for projects. There are two ways to do this and both of them have their advantages. Depending on the type of project you're doing, you may prefer one way over the other.

Using Ties as Ties

Everyone is always asking me why they can't make things out of ties without "harvesting" and washing them. Yes, you can, but because of the thickness of the tie, this is suggested for craft and quick projects only. This method uses the ties just as you found them and the interfacing and back of the tie are not removed. It is a quick technique and can result in an unplanned looking project because of the widely varied sizes and shapes of your ties. The project should definitely not be washed. With this method, less preparation is needed so the project goes faster. Also, the look is a bit "less flat" (close friends have described this as lumpy). I can not recommend this method. But other clever ways to use whole ties include weaving, braiding, fanning, wrapping.

My own special variation of this quickie technique allows you to remove the back and interfacing of the tie without changing its shape at all. This is demonstrated in "Easy Embellishments " Most ties, even cheap ones, have some sort of interfacing inside them. It's often a loosely-woven, "itchy" kind of interfacing. This often shrinks radically during washing, but don't despair, it is rarely stitched in and will automatically just fall out when you open the seam. Not being able to throw anything out, I've been saving this stuff and my garage is almost full of it. I haven't found a great use for this yet, but I've been told that there are some groups that weave rugs from it. The best thing that I can think of is that when you make a new tie for someone, you have the perfect interfacing to back it with. If you think of something better, I'd love to hear from you.

Using Ties as Fabric

All ties started out as just fabric, so all you are doing is returning them to their original state. Somehow this just seems environmentally correct and you can allow yourself to feel quite good about it. "Harvesting" tie fabric is what I love to call it. Others often refer to it as "gutting the ties." Whether you are harvesting or gutting, this requires a little extra work but is well worth doing because you can do a lot more things with the ties. The resulting projects are also flat, smooth and very professional-looking. They can not, however, be fondly referred to as "quick!" You will be taking the ties apart, washing them and pressing them flat. Ties, if totally useable, yield the equivalent of about 1/16th yard of fabric. As with fabric, you can then cut the "ties" into any shape or design that you like. This allows you to do patchwork, applique and just about any other sewing technique. I've found that it's not necessary to remove the linings at the point of the tie. This can be cut away later as you use them and why make more work for yourself? Also, there are the labels. Be sure to remove them carefully and save them. I've discovered some of the most colorful, silly and interesting labels during my tie harvests, but that's another book! Most of the projects in this book can be done by preparing your ties this way .

Should I Wash My Ties ?

Yes, dry cleaning is too expensive and washing makes them look fresher and smell much better. If they are clean and in good shape, I just go ahead and use them. But, generally, I like to wash the ties before using them. Especially if I don't know where they came from or they seem musty from being stored away somewhere. I conducted an informal mini-survey on how many men wash or have their ties cleaned. In the thousands of ties that I've used, I have only found one dry cleaning tag attached to the lining. Unless it was a very expensive tie, most men said that they wore them until they got dingy-looking and then just got a new one. That's great for you and me because it means that there are lots more ties out there for us to get our hands on.

Before getting into my washing techniques let me share some of my "dirty tie" experiences with you. I've discovered some very interesting stains on the ties that have come my way, some of which you really don't want to handle. But, I must say that I've never found one that was so bad that I couldn't use it. Keep in mind that if you wash your whole ties first, this always makes it harder to take out the stitching. Never throw the soiled or spotted ones away before you wash them. The classic gravy stain is probably the number one stain that I found, then marinara sauce is next and auto grease is a solid third place. The good news is that the staining can actually look interesting after the ties are washed, lending an antique patina to the surface of the fabric. The really bad stains never come out completely, but they leave a nice aged-looking tone to the fabric. I think that this is why so many of my quilts made from old ties are frequently mistaken for genuine antique quilts.

Here's what I found out after spending a few days in the basement, washing ties. On my first attempt, I impulsively dumped hundreds of ties into my washer and selected the delicate cycle. Why not? Sounds reasonable. I used cold water and a mild detergent. Not being a person who takes risks lightly, I then paced around nervously during the entire wash cycle because I just wasn't sure how this rash decision was going to turn out. I pictured myself ruining all my precious, irreplaceable ties. Where on earth was I going to get more ties? Why didn't I test this on just a few ties first? (I'm not going to answer that.) When the wash cycle was completed, the ties were all mixed together. You noticed I didn't use the words "tangled" or "knotted permanently", which might be a more accurate description. If you do it this way, you must remove them carefully, one at a time, gently separating them as you would do with long hair after washing it. (That sounds nice doesn't it?) Well, it isn't so nice. There I was, standing in my dark, unfinished basement, leaning over the washer, trying to unravel ties for about an hour. Out of frustration, I just threw them in the dryer and found that the high heat was much too hard on the delicate fabrics. Now I had a real case of "fabric abuse" on my hands. Not to mention the much larger, now damp and even tighter knot that I eventually had to undo after I calmed down.

For my next batch of ties, I completely hand ripped the ties open first before washing them. That just produced lots of very frayed edges, not to mention the precious wasted inches of fabric lost. There's not much fabric in a tie to start with so

this was a real mistake. Also, after removing the ties from the washer, there were millions, yes millions, of tiny silky threads that completely coated the inside of the washer. And you have never seen such an incredible knot. Avoid this mistake at all costs.

The Best Way to Wash Ties

Undiscouraged, convinced there was a better way and being a true subscriber to the scientific method, I proceeded to try another way. Working with only a handful of ties, say a dozen at a time maybe, hand-washing is definitely the answer. Open the back of the ties first and remove the interfacing. It's always seemed strange to me that the more expensive the tie, the easier it is to open. I always think of more expensive items being sewn together better. This is usually because a finely-made tie is delicately hand-stitched or loosely tacked with great care, and silk thread. Cheaper ties often have machine-made seams done with tiny stitches that are almost impossible to rip. It's not worth wasting the time to rip these, just cut the fabric closely along the seamline. Use a "fine-washables" detergent and cold water. You could use about 1/2 to 1/3 of the suggested amount of your regular detergent, but definitely avoid anything with bleach or other nasty chemicals. Swish the ties around in the water, let them soak for about ten minutes, rinse several times and line-dry indoors.

After the ties are line-dried, you

need to press them flat from the wrong side. Don't panic, some of them will look hopelessly wrinkled but I haven't come across many that aren't salvageable. This process can also bring out the worst in some badly-worn ties. If they've been stored in the basement, the moisture has probably attacked and weakened the fibers. This is sometimes not apparent until you've washed them. I've had a few ties just disintegrate in the wash, but this is good because at least you didn't include them in your project and find out the bad news later after the project's finished. Washing also serves other purposes, besides cleaning. Pre-shrinking is always an important step in any sewing project. Also, there are the amazing variety of "scents" that ties seem to pick up. In my studio, I have come to refer to this as "tie-aroma therapy" and guessing the source of the smells has resulted in several lengthy bouts of giggling amongst my helpers. Now, don't

My Tie Diary

How I washed my ties:

How it turned out:

saving them, before I make projects. There are lots of fun ways to use these and you won't even have to remove the lining. Tie points are a little different than Prairie Points but can be used in the same way. They make great zig-zag edge treatment for pillows and quilts. My favorite pillow is just rows and rows of tie points sewn to a backing in a wonderful, colorful arrangement resembling roof shingles or fish scales. Sounds like a great idea for a vest too!

with microscopic stitches so do this very carefully to keep from making a hole in the tie. You might want to start saving the labels for a future "label" project.

2) Beginning at the wider end of the tie, use a seam ripper to open the end of the seam. Sometimes there is a thread bar-tack at this point that you need to remove first. Put your thumb and your first finger inside the tie and spread it open. Locate the first stitch of the seam and start ripping. If the tie has been loosely hand stitched with silk thread, you possibly can easily pull it out in one piece. Use your ripper to cut the first stitch at each end of the tie and pull one end of the thread, as if you were gathering the tie, until the thread is completely removed. If the seam must be ripped, insert your thumb and forefinger into the tie and apply pressure from inside as you proceed.

3) Open the tie and remove the interfacing. It should come right out. Save this, ...if you must.

think that we're a bunch of tie sniffers! It's just that when you press your ties, the trapped aromas absorbed by the ties just come wafting up from the ironing board. Some of my favorites include Old Spice, cedar trunk, and aged wine. Other recognizable ones you might come across are moth balls, cigars, cigarettes, and beer. One I encounter frequently is Beef Wellington or maybe it's "something" in the recipe. I love surprises and discovering one that smelled distinctively like Play Dough *tm was really fun. Figure that one out! You will be glad to know that washing your ties almost completely removes any trace of these aromas, but the ironing isn't nearly as much fun!

Tie Tips

I've gotten into the habit of cutting off both tips of my ties first and

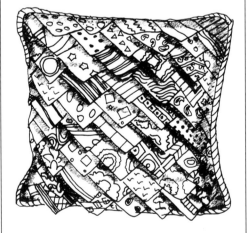

How to Take Apart a Tie

1) Turn the tie over so the seam on the back is facing you. Locate the label if there is one and remove it first. Sometimes these are sewn in

🎀 Cutting Your Tie Fabric

1) For very silky ties, there are several ways to "tame" them before cutting. Spray starch is my favorite way and it works great! Just spray the fabric lightly from the wrong side and iron dry. If you want it to be stiffer, simply repeat this again. Iron-on interfacing is another way to add body to limp fabrics and make them easier to use. Using the tie fabric as a pattern, cut a piece of interfacing to match and apply it to the wrong side following the manufacturer's directions. If you prefer, cut your shapes out first and then baste 100 % cotton muslin or flannel to the wrong side. Since ties are usually made on the bias grain, cut the backing fabric on the straight grain to stabilize it even further.

TIP: *To protect your iron and ironing board from stray fuser, I make a white tissue paper sandwich with my project in the middle.*

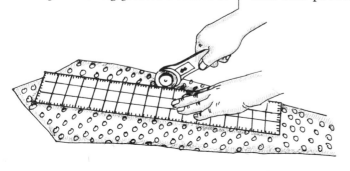

2) Layer the ties for cutting whenever possible. Pin the layers together as needed and use your rotary cutter to save time.

3) Store the cut pieces flat to keep them from fraying. Sort them in small plastic bags, by shape or color. To prevent wrinkles, roll whole ties up or hang them on a clothes drying rack. I have a row of shoe boxes full of ties, labeled by color for easy selection. One of them is marked "real uglies" and I save really obnoxious ones in there for special projects.

4) Sometimes silks and synthetic tie fabrics create a lot of static. I keep a wet sponge nearby so I can dampen my fingertips to reduce static whenever it becomes a problem. You can also use a plant mister to lightly spray the fabrics and the ironing board while you're working.

🎀 Pressing Matters

If you're not familiar with pressing delicate fabrics, there are only a few things to know. Use a silk setting on your iron and a little steam. You can prevent "bruising" and shiny spots on the fabric surface by A L W A Y S pressing from the wrong side. To prevent compressing the fibers with the iron, avoid putting any pressure on the iron. Heat will set creases and stains, so wash first. For really bad wrinkles, wash first and then iron dry, or use a plant mister to wet the fabric thoroughly. For pressing a completed project or piece of patchwork, use a press cloth to protect the right side of the fabric and use more steam than pressure. If you're unsure, test your technique on a scrap of similar fabric. The best methods for pressing seam allowances vary and are always a hot topic in sewing circles. They can be pressed open or in one direction and I feel that the choice should be based on your personal preference. Generally, I like to use the method that produces the neatest, most flat results. This can vary with the project, and I have sometimes suggested the way that I used to make the project, but always use your own favorite pressing method.

My Tie Diary

Ideas that I have for my ties:

Some sketches so I don't forget:

My Tie Diary

Photo of my favorite tie wearer:

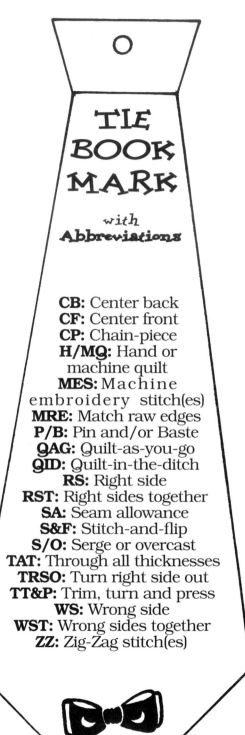

TIE BOOK MARK

with Abbreviations

CB: Center back
CF: Center front
CP: Chain-piece
H/MQ: Hand or machine quilt
MES: Machine embroidery stitch(es)
MRE: Match raw edges
P/B: Pin and/or Baste
QAG: Quilt-as-you-go
QID: Quilt-in-the-ditch
RS: Right side
RST: Right sides together
SA: Seam allowance
S&F: Stitch-and-flip
S/O: Serge or overcast
TAT: Through all thicknesses
TRSO: Turn right side out
TT&P: Trim, turn and press
WS: Wrong side
WST: Wrong sides together
ZZ: Zig-Zag stitch(es)

Sewing & Quilting Abbreviations

Knitters and crocheters have always used abbreviations to save space and make the instructions easier to follow. Why shouldn't there be some abbreviations for sewers and quilters? Spelling the same terms out over and over again just takes up too much space. So to make room for more projects, I've used the following abbreviations throughout the instructions. Someone has suggested that this innovation might drive you crazy, so I have given it to you in the form of a bookmark to use as easy reference wherever you are in the book. Just make a photo copy and glue it to cardboard, then punch a hole and add a tassel if you're really into it.

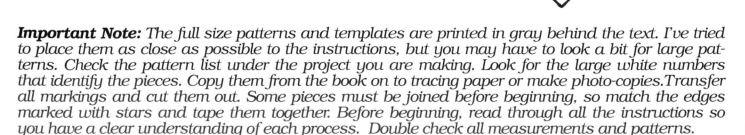

Important Note: *The full size patterns and templates are printed in gray behind the text. I've tried to place them as close as possible to the instructions, but you may have to look a bit for large patterns. Check the pattern list under the project you are making. Look for the large white numbers that identify the pieces. Copy them from the book on to tracing paper or make photo-copies. Transfer all markings and cut them out. Some pieces must be joined before beginning, so match the edges marked with stars and tape them together. Before beginning, read through all the instructions so you have a clear understanding of each process. Double check all measurements and patterns.*

CHAPTER 3

Patch-work Designs to Make with Tie Fabrics

This chapter includes the basic techniques that I used to create the tie projects in this book. I have adapted conventional methods to make working with ties easier. These include working over a base fabric using a S&F technique, stiffening with spray starch and stabilizing with lightweight fusible interfacing. You can use any of these to make pieces of "patchwork tie fabric" for the projects. This is a project book, packed with as much basic sewing and quilting information as possible. If you are a beginner or want more details, you might want to refer to a book on basic sewing and quilting techniques that focuses on lots more technical stuff. There are lots of wonderful books to choose from that have been written to teach you highly specialized and time saving sewing "arts'" such as rotary cutting, machine embroidery, and fine couturier techniques. I have suggested a few titles in the Source List.

Note: All cutting measurements given are exact. The final measurements of your projects may differ slightly due to variations in seam allowances, quilting take-up and individual workmanship.

LOG CABIN

The Log Cabin design is a good one for your first patchwork tie project. It always seems to look great, no matter how you put the different tie fabrics together. Whether you use a scissors or rotary cutter, this technique utilizes the tie fabrics really well. Working over a flannel base square allows you to QAG and makes the tie fabrics easier to manage.

Cutting Templates: All pieces include 1/4"(6 mm) SA
  A - Center Square
  B - Strip 1
  C - Strips 2 & 3
  D - Strips 4 & 5
  E - Strips 6 & 7
  F - Strips 8 & 9
  G - Strips 10 & 11
  H - Strips 12 & 13
  I - Strips 14 & 15
  J - Strip 16

Note: To divide the block diagonally into light and dark areas or different color families, cut the strips as follows:

  Light colors - Strips 1, 2, 5, 6, 9, 10, 13 & 14
  Dark colors - Strips 3, 4, 7, 8, 11, 12, 15 & 16

Shirley says: "When using the same template to cut light and dark pieces, layer them and cut both out at the same time."

Basic Steps:
1) Work the patchwork on a 7-1/2"x7-1/2" (19cm x 19cm) cotton flannel base square. Fold the square diagonally in both directions and press creases along the folds.

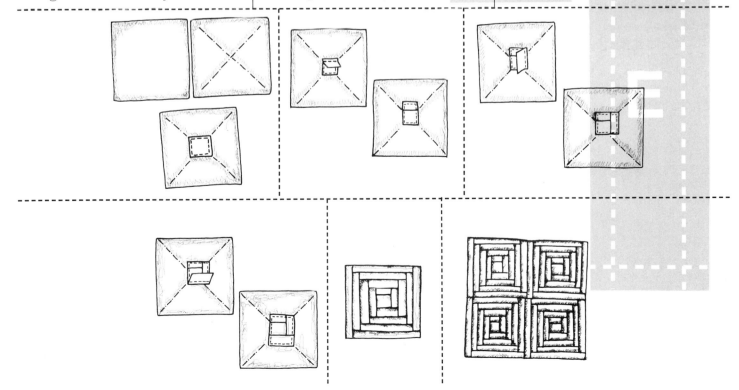

Mark the top of the square with a "T".

2) Place A on the flannel so that the corners are lined up with the diagonal creases. P/B it in place.

3) RST, place the first patchwork strip (B) at the top of the center square. MRE and stitch TAT. Press the strip over toward the outer edge of the base square and P/B the free edges of the strip to the base square.

4) RST, match the long edge of the second strip(C) to the right side of the center square, over the seam. MRE and stitch, press and P/B as before.

5) RST, match the long edge of the third strip to the bottom edge of the center square, over the seam. MRE and stitch, press and P/B as before.

6) Working in a clockwise direction, continue adding strips one at a time in alphabetical and numerical order until the base square is covered.

Shirley says: *"Because the tie fabrics are not straight grain, they may stretch causing some pieces to become slightly narrower in width than others. Don't fuss over this, just add more log cabin pieces so the base square is completely covered."*

7) Check the project directions for colors, size and the number of blocks needed for your project. Lay out the blocks to make your design. Seam them together into rows and then join the rows, matching the seams of the blocks.

GRANDMA'S FAN

The Grandma's Fan design is a great one to use if you don't have lots of tie fabrics. You can repeat the same fabric order in each fan and then use yardage for the fan centers and backgrounds. Working over a straight-grain background square of fabric helps control the bias tie fabrics. Equally pretty done by hand or machine, the seams can be embellished with embroidery stitches.

Cutting Templates:
A1 - Grandma's Fan Wedge
    1/4 " [6mm] SA
B1 - Grandma's Fan Center
    1/4" [6mm] SA
C1 - Grandma's Fan Placement
    guide

Note: The Grandma's Fan block looks best on a fabric base square of a solid color. Cut the six fan wedges from different tie fabrics. Cut all the fan centers for one project from the same fabric to avoid a too-busy look.

Shirley Says: "To quilt-as-you-go, P/B a piece of cotton flannel to the WS of the base square before beginning."

Basic Steps:
1) Make a pressing guide for the fan wedge by transferring A1 to thin cardboard and trimming off the SA at the wider curved end. Align the sides and narrow ends of the press-ing guide on the WS of the fabric fan piece. Press the SA over the wide curved edge of the cardboard, then remove it and press flat. Repeat on all fan wedges.

2) Use the Placement Guide (C1) to transfer the two curved lines to the background square.

3) P/B the first fan wedge to the background square so the pressed edge is even with the large curve. MRE at the edge of the background square.

4) RST, place the second fan wedge over the first. Match the pressed edges exactly. MRE along the sides of the fan wedges and stitch TAT. Press the fan wedge over and P/B the free edges to the background square. Repeat with the remaining four fan wedges.

Shirley Says: "Trim the corner of each pressed SA off diagonally before you S&F to eliminate bulk."

5) Make a pressing guide for the fan center as for the fan wedge. Trim the SA off of the curved edge. Press the curved edge of the fabric to the wrong side as before. Clip the SA to lie flat if necessary.

6) P/B the fan center to the corner of the fan. MRE to the background square. Applique the pressed edge so it covers the raw edges of the fan wedges. Use a slip stitch or MES. Also slipstitch or MES outer curved edge of fan. Add rows of contour quilting to the background, spaced 1/4" [6mm] to 1"(2.5 cm) apart.

7) Check the project directions for

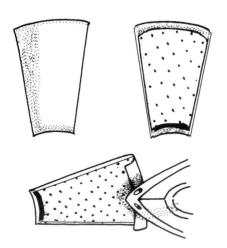

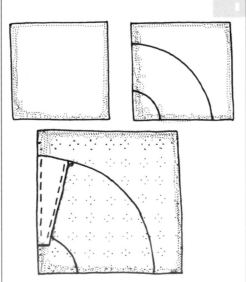

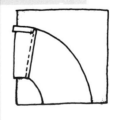

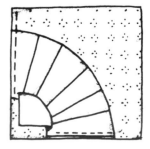

colors and the number of blocks needed for your project. Lay out the blocks to make your design. Seam them together into rows and then join the rows, matching the intersecting seams of the blocks.

◨◧ DRESDEN PLATE

The Dresden Plate design is a "cousin" of the Grandma's Fan design. The technique is very similar because you work on a background square and S&F Dresden Plate wedges around a circle. If you have lots of ties, cut each wedge from a different one. For less ties, repeat the same four, in the same sequence, around the circle.

Cutting Templates:
A2 - Dresden Plate Wedge - 1/4"(6 mm) SA
B2 - Dresden Plate Center Guide

Note: The circle at the center of the Dresden Plate is the fabric background square showing through. Select colors that coordinate and if necessary, add solid color fabrics wedges to avoid a "too-busy" look.

Basic Steps:
1) Make a pressing guide for the wedge by transferring A2 to thin cardboard and trimming off the SA's at the inner curve and the pointed end. Align the long sides of the pressing guide on the WS of the fabric plate wedge. Press the SA over the cardboard, clipping as needed at the curve. Press one side of the point over first, and then the other to get a nice flat point.
2) Fold the background square into quarters and press creases at each

fold. Transfer the outline of the the center circle B2 to the middle of the square.
3) P/B the first plate wedge to the background square so the pressed, curved edge is on the circle and one raw edge overlaps the creaseline by 1/4"
4) Working clockwise, RST, place the second plate wedge over the first. Match the pressed edges exactly. MRE along the sides of the plate wedge and stitch TAT. Press the plate section over and P/B the free edges to the background square. Repeat with the remaining plate wedges to complete the circle. Place four wedges between the creaselines in each quarter of the Dresden Plate design.

Shirley says: "As you stitch each plate section in place, use a MES to embellish the seamline and finish the edges. Beginning at the unstitched side, stitch across the center curve, up the finished seam and around the pointed edge Then add the next wedge and repeat..

5) To finish the last plate wedge, press under the SA on the side that will overlap the raw edge where you started. Use a slip stitch or MES to secure the pressed edges around the circle and the outer points. Add rows of contour quilting to the background. as desired

◨◧ CRAZY CHUNKS

This Crazy Chunks design allows you to use up all the odd-shaped scraps. The possibilities are unlimited and no two blocks ever look the same. Using satins and fancy fabric

to mix with your tie fabrics looks great and helps you fill in any hard-to-fit areas, when you don't have a scrap large enough. Hand or machine embroidery decorates the seams and makes it easy to hide any problem spots.

Note: Lay out all your leftover fabric scraps. Select pieces 3"(7.5 cm) wide or larger for the best results. Use an assortment of contrasting colors and shapes. Straight edges are easier to work with than curves, until you get a little practice.

Basic Steps:

1) Cut a cotton flannel base piece large enough for your project. Fold it diagonally in both directions and press creases along the folds. Cut a matching piece of paper, folding it same way.
2) Working over the paper, plan your design as if you where working a puzzle. With the RS up, put the first piece in the center and continue placing the fabrics scraps

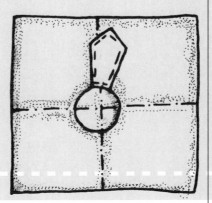

around it in a clockwise manner. Try to match the edges of each new piece to the spaces created by previous ones. Experiment with the placement of color and texture. The raw edges of the pieces should overlap by at least 3/4"(2 cm) to allow for a SA and slight adjustments. Trim the larger scraps down to fit as necessary. For covering large areas, add several rounds of chunks around the center. Cover the paper completely, pinning each piece down.

3) PB the center piece over the intersection of the creases in the middle of the flannel, positioning it just like it was on the paper.

4) Working clockwise, transfer and stitch each piece one at a time from the paper to the flannel base. RST, stitch each new piece to the edge of the previous one TAT. Press it over in place and P/B the free edges to the flannel.

Shirley says: *"To get accurately fitting pieces, press under the SA on each piece and test it before stitching it down."*

5) When adding a piece that forms a corner, press under the SA on the adjacent edge before stitching it in place. Sometimes, an adjoining piece can also be tucked underneath. After the pressed edge is flipped over in place, hand or machine stitch it down.

6) To finish the edge of the last piece, press under the SA so it covers all raw edges. Trim off any excess fabric even with the base square.

7) Embellish the seams of the crazy chunks with hand or MES.

CRAZY STRIPS

This Crazy Strips design makes great use of your ties with a minimum of cutting and seaming. The bias grain of the ties allows you to get great results when placing the seams at different odd angles. You can work with scraps or complete ties, using straight or diagonal seams. Each completed piece will be unique. Just seam one narrow tie end to another narrow one, and

the wide ones to each other.

Note: *Use various lengths cut from different ties to create these random strips. After removing the tie points, stitch the tie sections into one continuous piece using diagonal seams. Match the tie widths as close as possible at the seams. Trim the long raw edges so they are even. Thencut the entire length in half.*

Shirley says: *"For a more intentional look, add machine embroidery to the tie seams before joining the strips, and then use a different stitch to embellish the long seams."*

Note: *Straight strips 1" - 3"(2.5 cm - 7.5 cm) wide can be used for this technique as well. You can use one width throughout or assorted widths.*

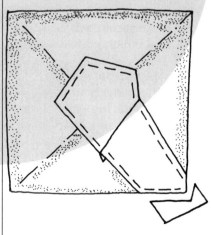

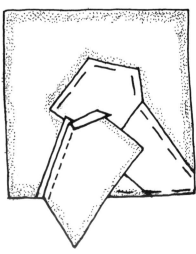

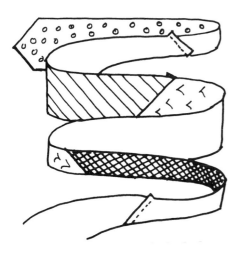
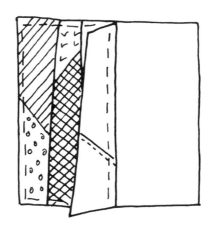

Basic Steps:

1) Work the crazy strips on any size cotton flannel base piece. P/B the tie strip to the edge of the flannel.

Shirley Says: *For straight strips on the diagonal, fold a square diagonally and press a crease along the fold. P/B the first strip along the crease-line. Trim it off even with the base piece.*

2) RST, place a second strip on top of the first. MRE and stitch TAT. Press the strip over and P/B the free edges of the strip to the base piece.

3) Working from one side to the other, continue adding strips until the base piece is covered. If using diagonal straight strips, repeat until you reach the corner of the base piece. Continue at the strip where you started, covering the other side of the base piece as before.

⧓ BOW TIE

This Bow Tie design is one that I just had to include even though it seems challenging to do with tie fabrics. The innovative S&F technique that I came up with makes it easy to do with ties and eliminates the tricky inset corners. The muslin base square keeps the small pieces under control. Cutting the background pieces from straight-grain fabric allows you to make crisp corners and straight edges.

Cutting Templates: 1/4"
(6 mm) SA included

A3 - Bow Tie Background & Tie Sections
B3 - Bow Tie Knot
C3 - Bow Tie Base Square with placement guidelines

Note: *The Bow Tie blocks are done on a muslin base square. The Knot and Tie Sections for one block are cut from matching tie fabric. Each block features a different tie fabric. The backgrounds are cut from solid colors.*

Basic Steps:

1) Make a pressing guide for the Background/Tie Section by transferring A3 to thin cardboard and trimming off the SA's on the two short sides, adjacent to the diagonal side.

2) Work each block on a muslin base square. Fold the square into quarters and press creases along the folds.

3) Place the Bow Tie Knot diagonally on the muslin so that the corners are lined up with the creases. P/B the knot in place.

4) RST, place one Tie Section (A3) at one side of the knot. MRE and stitch TAT. Press the section over so the long straight edges match the corner of the base square. Avoid removing the creases from the muslin. P/B the free edges to the muslin. Repeat this with the second tie section on the opposite side of the knot.

5) Align the long straight sides of the pressing guide to those on the WS of one background piece. Press the SA's over the cardboard, then remove it and press flat. Repeat this with second background.

6) RST, place one background at one raw edge of the knot. MRE and align the pressed sides with both seams on the knot. S&F as before. P/B the background TAT so the raw edges of the tie are covered and the pressed edges match the crease-lines on the muslin. Repeat this with the second background on the opposite side of the knot.

7) Use a slipstitch or MES to secure the pressed edges in place. Start stitching at one edge of the block, pivot and stitch across the knot. Pivot again and stitch to the other edge of the block. The background piece will look like it's outlined with stitches.

Shirley says: *"Use gray thread and the machine 'blind hem stitch' or 'heirloom applique stitch' to finish the edge of the background pieces. Adjust the stitch width and length so it looks like tiny hand applique stitches."*

8) Check the project directions for colors and the number of blocks needed. Arrange the blocks, directing the Bow Ties as desired. Seam them together into rows and then join the rows, matching the seams and Bow Ties where they intersect.

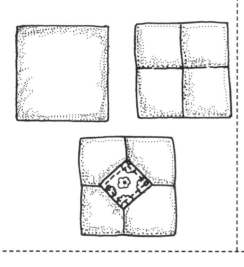
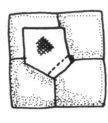

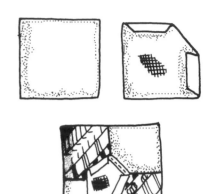

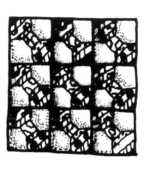

🎀 LONE STAR

The Lone Star design looks so good when done with ties, I just couldn't omit it. Bias, silky tie fabrics in a variety of weights was not going to stop me. Not recognized as an "easy" one to do, my method shows you how to stabilize the diamonds with very lightweight, fusible interfacing before putting them together. This also gives body to the pieces, makes them all uniform in weight and defines the SA at the same time.

Cutting Templates:
A4 - Lone Star Diamond - 1/4"(6 mm) SA
B4 - Lone Star Stabilizer

*Note: The Lone Star is a challenging design to do with tie fabrics. This technique helps control both the slippery fabrics and the accuracy required for piecing. Each diamond is backed with a fusible stabilizer piece that defines the stitchline. Individual diamonds are first joined into rows and then into a large dia-*mond section. Eight sections are combined to make the Lone Star. The fabrics are arranged in a sequence that creates radiating rounds of color.

Basic Steps:
1) Using a very soft pencil, draw the needed number of stabilizer shapes on the non-fusible side of the lightweight interfacing. Draw a straight line across the interfacing to start. Place the diamonds next to each other so they share a common cutting line. Cut them out.
2) Working on the wrong side of your fabrics, fuse the fusible side of the stabilizer pieces to the tie fabrics leaving a full 1/4"(6 mm) all around each piece. Draw the SA around each diamond or use a rotary cutter and ruler to measure and cut simultaneously. Cut out all the required colors of diamonds for the project. Avoid stitching the pieces.
3) Lay out the diamonds for one Lone Star section. Following the layout carefully, stitch the diamonds together into rows. Press the seams in one direction.

Shirley says: "Press the SA's of adjoining rows of patchwork in opposite directions so matching the points is easier. When machine stitching, hold the seam so the SA's are directed towards the presser foot."

4) Lay out the rows for one section. RST, stitch the rows together, matching the patchwork seams. Press. Repeat this to make a total of eight sections.
5) Lay out all the sections to make the Lone Star. P/B two sections together, placing RST and matching the patchwork seams. Beginning at the center, stitch the seam, stopping at the outer edge where the SA's intersect. Press. Repeat this to make four combined sections.

Shirley says: "Press all the seams for both halves of the star in exactly the same way, then join the two halves, pressing the center seam in one direction. After stitching, trim away the corners of the SA's wherever possible to eliminate bulk."

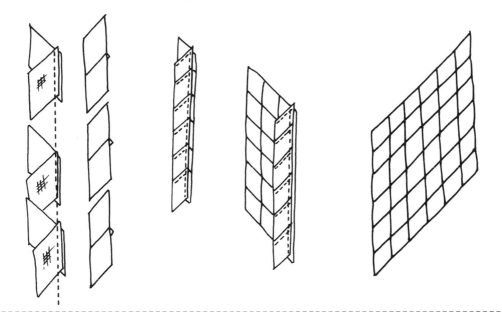

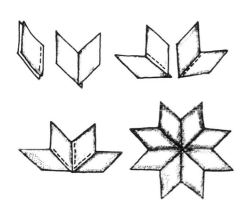

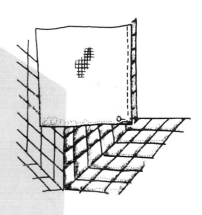

6) Lay out all the combined sections. P/B two of them together to make a half star. Beginning at the center, stitch the seam as before. Press. Repeat this to make the second half.

7) Join the two halves of the star in the same way. Press.

8) Lay out the star and make patterns for the background pieces. P/B a square in each corner of the star, RST. MRE at the outer point of the star and stitch towards the center of the star, stopping in the corner where you ended the seams between the sections. Stitch the adjacent side of the square in the same way. Press. Repeat to insert all four background squares.

9) Insert the background triangles in the same way. Press.

HEXAGON HONEY-COMB

The Hexagon Honeycomb design is a versatile one that can be used to make patchwork "tie fabric" to use for almost any project. Each hexagon is backed with very lightweight, fusible interfacing so it's easy to work with and also marks the SA. Individual pieces can be joined by hand or machine. This is a great one to take along with you if you enjoy doing handwork. If your collection of ties is all in one color-coordinated family, hexagons will show them off really well.

Cutting Templates:
A5 - Hexagon - 1/4"(6 mm) SA
B5 - Hexagon Stabilizer

Note: Hexagons can be joined by

hand or machine. Each hexagon is backed with a fusible stabilizer piece that defines the stitchline. Individual hexagons are first joined into rows and then into a large section.

Basic Steps:
1) Using a very soft pencil, draw the needed number of stabilizer shapes on the non-fusible side of the lightweight interfacing. Draw a straight line across the interfacing to start. Place the hexagons next to each other so they share a common cutting line. Cut them out.

2) Working on the wrong side of your fabrics, fuse the fusible side of the stabilizer pieces to the tie fabrics leaving a full 1/4"(6 mm) all around each piece. Draw the SA around each hexagon or use a rotary cutter and ruler to measure and cut simultaneously. Cut out all the required colors of hexagons for the

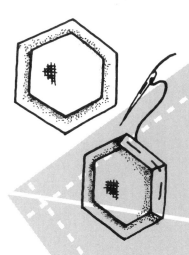

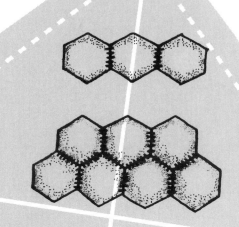

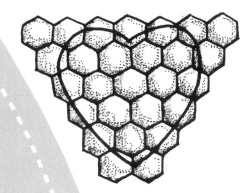

project.

3) Working around the first hexagon in one direction, press the SA to the wrong side. The crease will occur along the edge of the interfacing. Fold the corners in neatly as you press the next side. Continue in the same way around the hexagon, until all edges are pressed. If the SA's do not stay flat, P/B them in place.

Shirley says: *"Lay out your different-colored hexagons so they make a design like a flower, a stripe or a flame-stitch pattern."*

4) Lay out the hexagons into your design. Following the layout carefully, stitch the hexagons together into rows. Only opposite sides of each hexagon are stitched together. By hand: RST, match the edges of the hexagons and use a whip stitch on the wrong side to join. By machine: RS up, butt the sides of the hexagons together and work a ZZ or MES over the seam. Press.

5) Lay out the rows of hexagons and join them as before. Match the edges of two rows and stitch them together in one continuous zig zag seam.

A6

B6

Chapter 4:

ACCES-SORIES

 **SIX-TIE SCARF**

Finished size: About 12" x 65"(30.5 cm x 165 cm)

What you'll need:

Six ties in coordinated colors
Thread for construction

How to make it:

1) Open the tie seams and remove the interfacing. Press.

2) Working on the wider end of the tie, measure 28"(71 cm) along the side edge. Draw a line straight across the tie at this point and then cut off the narrower end. Repeat this on all the ties.

3) Using one tie as a pattern, trim the cut end of each tie to the same width. Then, trim both sides of the ties as needed, blending the trimmed end gradually into the side edge. Some ties will be wider than others.

4) The wide point of each tie is already finished. If your ties have a lining, rip the lining seams open at the side edges only. Press and baste the raw edges of the lining and the tie together.

5) RST, P/B three ties together along the side edges. Match the finished edges at the pointed ends. Stitch the seams and S/O. Repeat this to make a second scarf section.

6) RST, stitch the shorter ends of the two scarf sections together. P/B, matching the tie seams. S/O the seam. Press.

7) RST, fold the scarf in half lengthwise matching the wide points, raw edges and center seam. P/B the seam, stitch and finish as before. TRSO through one end. Press.

Shirley says: *"Dress things up by adding a bead and a tiny tassel to the pointed end of each tie. You'll need six beads and six tassels."*

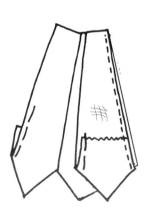

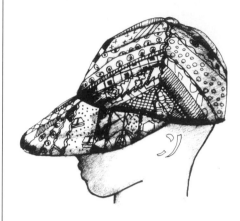

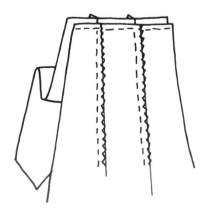 **HOME RUN HEAD-GEAR**

Finished size: Head sizes 20"-23"(51 cm - 58.5 cm)

What you'll need:

Tie fabrics - assorted scraps to equal 5/8 yard (0.60 m)
Flannel - 3/8 yard (0.40 m)
Heavy black satin - 3/8 yard (0.40 m)
Buckram - 1/4 yard (0.30 m)
Black grosgrain ribbon 1"(2.5 cm) wide - 7/8 yard (0.90 m)
Elastic 1/2"(1.3 cm) wide - 3-1/2"(9 cm)
Button to cover - 3/4"(2 cm)
Thread for construction and MES

Patterns:

A6 Crown section - 1/4"(6 mm) SA; with chevron placement guidelines
B6 Half brim - 1/4"(6 mm) SA

Pieces to cut:

Tie scraps - assorted strips 1" to 2"(2.5 cm to 5 cm) wide
Flannel - Six of A6; Two of B6
Satin - Six of A6; One of B6 placing dotted line on fabric fold
Buckram - Two of B6, placing dot ted line on fabric fold

Shirley says: "For easier and more accurate cutting of the lining and buckram, make a complete brim pattern. Cutting two B6 pieces from paper, trim the SA's off along the center straight edges and match and tape them together."

How to make it:

1) The patchwork creates a chevron design at each seam. Transfer the placement lines to the crown and brim flannel pieces so you have left and right pairs that will form a "V" when sewn together.

2) Beginning at the placement line, follow the Crazy Strips basics in Chapter 3 to cover all the flannel pieces with narrow tie strips. Embellish all the seams with MES.

3) Lay out the crown pieces in a row so they create a chevron design. RST, P/B the first two pieces together along one curved edge. Stitch and press the seam open. Embellish the seam with MES. Add the third crown piece in the same way. Join the remaining three pieces together to make a second half crown.

4) RST, stitch the two halves of the crown together. Press and embellish the seam as before.

5) Assemble the crown lining in the same way. WST, insert the lining into the crown and P/B the raw edges together.

6) Stitch the two buckram pieces together 3/8"(1 cm) in from all raw edges. Trim away 1/4"(6 mm) from all sides.

7) RST, stitch the brim sections together at the center seam. Press and embellish as for the crown seams. RST, P/B the brim lining to the brim around the outside curved edge. Stitch, TT&P. Insert the buckram in between the layers and P/B the inner curved edge, enclosing the buckram inside.

8) RST, match the center seam of the brim to one seam on the crown. MRE, P/B and stitch the brim to the edge of the crown.

9) P/B the grosgrain ribbon around the raw edges of the hat, overlapping the bottom edge 1/4"(6 mm). Press under the raw end and overlap them where they meet. Edgestitch the ribbon in place and press to the inside of the hat.

10) At the back of the hat, stitch a 3/4"(2 cm) wide casing for a distance of 4"(10 cm). Insert the elastic into the casing, tacking the ends and adjusting to fit.

11) Tack the free edge of the ribbon to the lining. Cover the button with tie fabric and tack to the top of the crown.

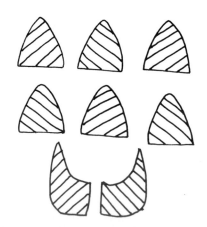

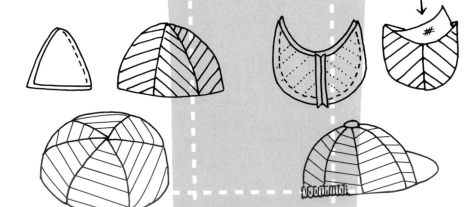

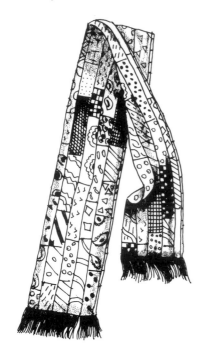

🎀 SCARF OF MANY COLORS

Finished size: 7-1/4" x 58"(18.5 cm x 148 cm) plus fringe

What you'll need:

Tie fabrics - assorted scraps to equal 3/4 yard (0.70 m)

Ivory, navy and wine silky blouse weight fabric - 1/4 yard (0.30 m) each

Black fringe 4"(10 cm) wide - one yard (0.9 m)

Thread for construction

Pieces to cut:

Cut all fabrics into 2"(5 cm) wide strips in various lengths from 1-1/2" to 6"(3.8 cm to 15 cm) long

How to make it:

1) RST, P/B the assorted color fabric rectangles into a 58"(148 cm) long strip. Stitch, S/O and press

the seams in one direction. Repeat this to make a total of ten strips.

2) RST, MRE of two strips and P/B them together. Stitch and S/O the seam. Repeat this to join all the strips.

3) P/B the top edge of the fringe to the RS on each short end of the scarf. Stitch.

4) RST, fold the scarf in half lengthwise. MRE, stitch and S/O the long edges together, keeping the fringe ends free. TRSO and press. Press the top edge of the fringe to the inside of the scarf and tack in place.

Shirley say's: *"This is a great way to use up all your leftovers. Make large pieces of scrap fabric for a vest."*

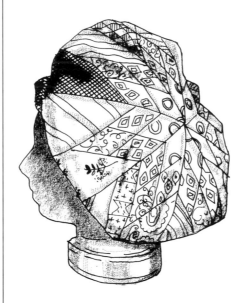

🎀 LONE STAR CHAPEAU

Finished Size: Head sizes 20" - 23"(51 cm - 58.5 cm)

What you'll need:

Three ties for the Lone Star in

crown

8-16 ties for the side sections

Lining - 3/4 yard (0.70 m)

Grosgrain ribbon 1"(2.5 cm) wide - 3/4 yard (0.70 m) for hat band

Elastic 1/2"(1.3 cm) wide - 8"(20.5 cm)

Thread for construction

Patterns:

A7 Lone Star diamond - 1/4"(6 mm) SA

B7 Side section - 1/4"(6 mm) SA

Pieces to cut:

Tie fabrics: For the Lone Star crown (A7) - Eight of color 1 (star center); Sixteen of color 2; Eight of color 3; For the side sections (B7) - eight lefts and eight rights in assorted colors

Lining: One 12"(30.5) circle; one 7" x 38-1/2"(18 cm x 98 cm) rectangle.

How to make it:

1) Follow the Lone Star basics in Chapter 3 to assemble the crown.

2) Arrange the side sections into a row with the straight ends even. RST, stitch the first two sections together along the longer seam, forming a point. Press the seam open.

3) P/B the next side section in place, matching the shorter sides. MRE and stitch, stopping at the point where the SA's intersect. Press the seam open. Repeat to join all the side sections into a row.

4) Join the side section into a cylinder by stitching the last seam.

5) Insert the Lone Star crown at the pointed edge of the joined sides.

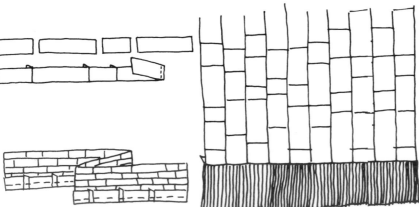

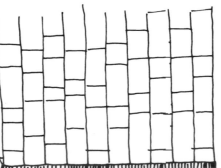

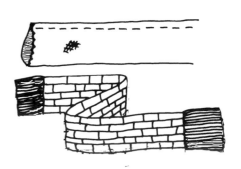

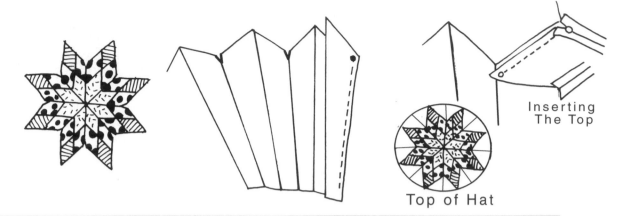

Top of Hat

Inserting The Top

RST, match the Lone Star points to the side indentations, not the points, of the side piece. P/B one section at a time, working from the side piece. Begin stitching at the indentation, matching the Lone Star SA to the unstitched part of the side seam. Stitch to the seamline at the point of the side. Turn the seam to match the Lone Star SA. Pivot and stitch towards the next Lone Star point.

6) Repeat Step 5 to completely attach the crown. Press the SA toward the side sections.

7) RST, match the two 7"(18 cm) sides of the lining and stitch. Fold one raw edge into quarters and mark with pins. Fold the circle into quarters and mark with pins. RST, P/B the circle to the lining, matching the quarter marks and easing as needed. Stitch and with WST, insert the lining into the hat and P/B the raw edges together.

8) P/B the grosgrain ribbon around the raw edges of the hat, overlapping the bottom edge 1/4"(6 mm). Press under the raw end and overlap them where they meet. Edgestitch the ribbon in place and press to the inside of the hat.

9) At the back of the hat, stitch a 3/4"(2 cm) wide casing for a distance of six side sections. Insert the elastic into the casing, tacking the ends and adjusting to fit. Tack the free edge of the ribbon to the lining.

POUF PURSE
Finished size: 8" x 12"(20.5 cm x 30.5 cm)

What you'll need:
Tie fabrics – assorted blacks/grays to equal 1/2 yard (0.50 m)
Gray taffeta - 5/8 yard (0.60 m)
    Interfacing - 3/8 yard (0.40 m) each
Cotton batting - 7" x 18"(18 cm x 45.5 cm)
Black piping - 3/8"(1 cm) - 1-1/4 yards (1.20 m)
Black cording 3/8"(1 cm) - 7/8 yards (0.90 m)
Snap closure
Thread for construction, quilting and MES

Patterns:
A8 Bag flap/insert - 1/4"(6 mm) SA with quilting design
B8 Half bag body - 1/4"(6 mm) SA

Pieces to cut:
Tie fabrics - Thirty-two 2" x 6"(5 cm x 15 cm) strips
Taffeta - Four of A8; three of B8

Interfacing - Two of B8
Batting - One of A8

How to make it:
1) RST, seam two tie rectangles together, matching the 6"(15 cm) edges. Repeat this to make a strip containing sixteen rectangles. Press the seams in one direction and embellish with MES. Make a second strip for the bag back in the same way.

2) Make two rows of gathering stitches, spaced 1/8" and 1/4"(3 mm and 6 mm) apart on all four long edges. Gather one side of each pieced strip up to fit the outer curved edge of the interfacing bag body. MRE and P/B the gathers to the interfacing. Gather the inner edge to fit around the placement line and P/B in place. Trim the interfacing away along the placement line. At the top four outer corners of the bag, place a small pleat 1"(2.5 cm) in from the raw edges. Direct the pleats towards the outer edges of the bag.

Shirley says: "When gathering, use a different color thread in your bobbin so the threads to pull are easier to see."

3) P/B piping around the insert edges of the front and back. Also apply piping around the outer edge of the bag front.

4) RST, baste the front insert into the bag front. Machine stitch, matching centers and easing around the curves. Repeat this for the back insert.

5) Transfer the quilting design to one flap piece, back with batting

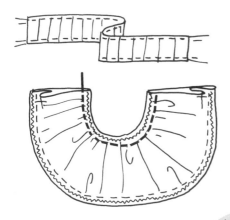

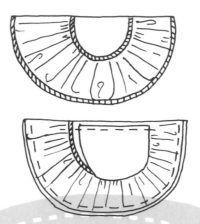

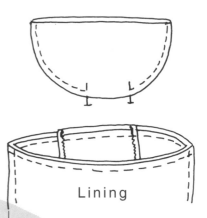

Lining

and H/MQ.

6) RST, stitch the flap lining to the quilted flap along the outer curved edge. TT&P, then baste the raw edges together. RST, P/B the flap to the back insert.

7) RST, P/B the bag front to the back. MRE and stitch around the outer curved edge. TRSO and tack the ends of the cord strap to each side of the flap on the bag back.

8) RST, stitch the lining front and back together along the curved edge, leaving a 6"(15 cm) opening to turn. Insert the bag into the lining, RST. P/B the entire top edge, matching the side seams. Stitch and TRSO through the opening. Press and understitch the upper edge. Slip stitch the opening closed.

9) Stitch the snap in place. Note: If you are using a magnetic bag snap, follow the manufacturer's instructions to install the parts of the snap before the bag is assembled.

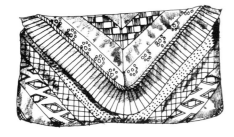

⬩ CLUTCH CLASSIC

Finished size: 7-1/2" x 13"(19 cm x 33 cm)

What you'll need:

Tie fabrics, velvet, satins - assorted reds & wine pieces 3-1/2" x 13"(9 cm x 33 cm) or larger to equal 5/8 yard (0.60 m)
Red taffeta - 5/8 yard (0.60 m)
Muslin - 3/8 yard (0.40 m)
Cotton batting - 15" x 22" (38 cm x 56 cm)
Burgundy piping - 5/8 yard (0.60 m)
Perfect Pleater
Snap closure
Thread for construction and MES

Pieces to cut:

Tie fabrics, velvets, satins - Cut pairs of strips, 1-1/2" x 12"(3.8 cm x 30.5 cm), totaling twenty-four pieces
Taffeta - Four 1-1/2" x 12"(3.8 cm x 30.5 cm) strips; two 7" x 20-1/2"(18 cm x 52 cm) lining pieces; one 3-1/2" x 54"(9 cm x 138 cm) ruffle strip
Muslin & batting - Two 7" x 20-1/2"(18 cm x 52 cm) pieces of each

How to make it:

1) Fold one corner of the 7" x 20-1/2"(18 cm x 52 cm) lining piece over at a 45 degree angle. Crease the fold and cut on the creaseline. RST, put the two lining pieces together and cut the second one using the first one as a pattern. Repeat this to cut the muslin and batting.

2) Baste the batting piece to the muslin. Beginning at the diagonal edge, follow the Crazy Strips basics in Chapter 3 to cover the batting/muslin with fabric strips.

Repeat this to make the other side of the clutch, using the fabrics in the same order so they will match at the center seam. Embellish each seam with MES.

Shirley says: *"Double check the width of each strip at the center seamline as you stitch them down to make sure they match accurately."*

3) RST, match the two pieced bag sections together so they form a pointed flap at one end. P/B, stitch and press the seam open.

4) Baste the piping to the diagonal edges of the flap.

5) WST, fold the ruffle strip in half lengthwise and crease the fold. Pleat the entire length of ruffle and secure it with stay stitching 1/4"(6 mm) from the raw edge. Baste the raw edge of the pleated ruffle to the flap edges, over the piping. Taper the ruffle at the side corners and trim off the excess.

6) Stitch the two lining sections together as you did for the clutch, leaving a 6" opening in the middle. RST, stitch the lining to the clutch at the end opposite the flap. Understitch the seam. Also, stitch them together at the flap end, starting and stopping 1-1/2"(3.8 cm) beyond the side corners of the flap. Clip the SA to the point where you stopped stitching.

7) RST, P/B the sides of the clutch and lining together. MRE, placing the finished front edge of the clutch at the point where you stopped stitching the flap. Stitch from the fold to the dot and repeat this on the lining. Do not catch the flap in the stitching.

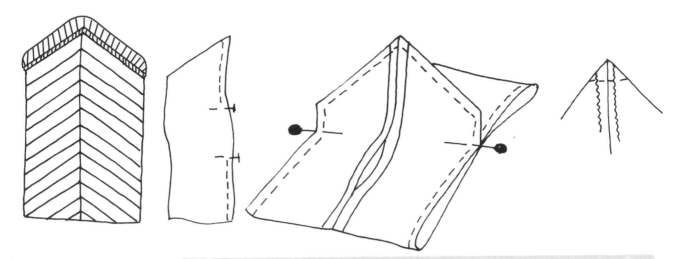

8) Make a boxed corner at the bottom of the clutch and the lining. Working from the wrong side, fold the bottom of the bag so the center of the bottom is aligned with the side seam. Measure up from the point 5/8"(1.5 cm) and draw a line perpendicular to the seam. Stitch on the line and trim the SA to 1/4"(6 mm). Repeat on the other side and lining corners.

9) Turn the clutch right side out through the lining opening. Press the lining to the inside and slip stitch the opening closed.

10) Stitch the snap in place. Note: If you are using a magnetic bag snap, follow the manufacturer's instructions to install the parts of the snap before the lining is closed.

Chapter 5:

GIFTS & GOODIES

◄►❓ TIE-LER THE TEDDY

Finished size: 20"(51 cm) tall

What you'll need:

Tie fabrics - Assorted blue/gray scraps to equal 2yards(1.90 m)

Blue taffeta - 5" x 14"(12.5 cm x 35.5 cm)

Flannel - 7/8 yard (0.90 m)

Cotton batting - 5" x 14"(12.5 cm x 35.5 cm)

Stuffing - 26 ounces (728 g)

Buttons for joints - Four 1"(2.5 cm); four 1/2"(1.3 cm)

Teddy bear eyes

Felt scrap - 1-1/2" x 2-1/2"(3.8 cm x 6.3 cm)

Ribbon 1-1/2"(3.8 cm) wide - One yard (1.0 m)

Long Doll Needle & heavy thread

Thread for construction & MES

Patterns:

A9 Body front - 1/4"(6 mm) SA; Dots for ear and eyes (Join two pattern pieces matching stars)

B9 Body back - 1/4"(6 mm) SA; Dots for opening;(join 2 pattern pieces matching stars)

C9 Arm - 1/4"(6 mm) SA; Cut line indicated for inner arms;dots for joint placement

D9 Leg - 1/4"(6 mm) SA;dot for joint placement

E9 Ear - 1/4"(6 mm) SA

F9 Paw - 1/4"(6 mm) SA; Quilting lines indicated

G9 Foot - 1/4"(6 mm) SA; Quilting lines indicated

Pieces to cut:

Flannel - Two 20" x 26"(51 cm x 66 cm) base pieces

Taffeta & batting - Two of F9; Two of G9

How to make it:

1) Follow the Crazy Chunks basics in Chapter 3 to cover both flannel base pieces with tie scraps. Embellish the seams with MES.

Shirley says; "Pick your favorite technique to make the teddy bear. The Log Cabin, Crazy Chunks, Crazy Strips, Bow Tie, Lonestar, and Honeycomb techniques could be used to cover the base square."

2) RST, pin the two Crazy Chunk pieces together. Lay out the teddy bear pieces - A9, B9, Outer arm C9 Inner arm C9, two D9 and two E9 - on the pinned pieces. Cut them out through both layers so you have left and right pieces. Staystitch the raw edges of all the teddy bear pieces before you begin.

3) RST, P/B two ear pieces together. Stitch the curved edge and TT&P. MRE and gather the straight edge into 2-3/4"(7 cm). Gather the top of the head between the dots to the same measurement and baste the ear to the head. Repeat to make the other ear.

4) RST, P/B the body fronts together at the CF seam and stitch. Make darts in the body back. RST, P/B the body backs together at the CB seam, leaving an opening at the dots for stuffing. Machine stitch and press SA's in opposite directions.

5) RST, P/B the body front to the back. Machine stitch and TT&P. Stuff and slip stitch the opening closed.

Shirley says: "Add pellets to the stuffing in the lower section of the body to add weight and make the bear sit up better."

6) Transfer the quilting lines to the RS of the taffeta paw pieces. Baste the batting pieces to the WS of the taffeta paws and quilt. RST, stitch the paws to the inner arm pieces along the straight ends so they match the shape of the outer arm. RST, P/B the inner arm to the outer arm, leaving an opening between the dots to stuff. TT&P, then stuff the arm and slip stitch the opening closed. Repeat this to make the other arm.

7) Transfer the quilting lines to the RS of the taffeta foot pieces. Baste the batting to the WS of the taffeta feet and quilt.

8) RST, P/B two leg sections together and stitch, leaving an opening to stuff. P/B the foot to the open end of the leg, matching the heel and toe to the seams. Stitch, clip curves, TT&P, then stuff the leg and slip stitch the opening closed. Repeat this to make the other leg.

9) Attach the arms and legs to the body with the doll needle, heavy thread and the buttons. Place the large button on the outside of the arms and legs and the small button between the arm and the body. Center them in the shoulder area of the arm and the hip area of the leg. Stitch the two buttons together through the stuffing so they squeeze it together. Insert the doll needle through the body at the shoulder joint to the other side. Pass the needle through the arm buttons and back through the body to the other side several times. Secure the end by wrapping the thread around the small button as you would for a button shank and knot it. Repeat on the opposite arm. Attach the legs in the same way.

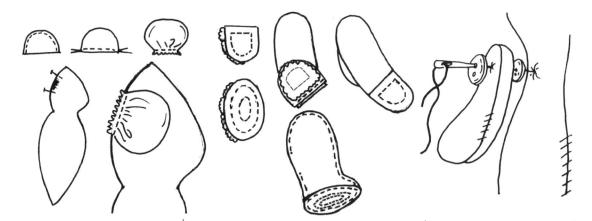

Shirley says: *"You can use 1-1/2"(3.8 cm) diameter doll joints to attach the arms and legs instead of buttons. Follow the manufacturer's instructions to insert them before finishing the stuffing and closing the openings.*

10) Cut two 1"(2.5 cm) circles from the felt. Use a pinking shears to shape eyelashes around about three-quarters of each circle. Glue the felt eyelashes to the back of each eye and attach the eyes at the marks. Tie bow.

🎀 TIE-RANNOSAURUS-REX

Finished size: 15"(38 cm) tall

What you'll need:

Tie fabrics - Assorted greens to equal 1-1/2 yards (1.40 m)

Lightweight fusible interfacing - 2-3/4 yards (2.60 m)

Red lame' - 1/8 yard (0.20 m)

Flannel - One yard (1.00 m)

Stuffing - 26 ounces (728 g)

Teddy bear eyes

Felt scrap - 1-1/2" x 2-1/2"(3.8 cm x 6.3 cm)

Green thread for construction and MES
14"(35.5 cm) pet collar and leash

Small pearls by the yard for mouth-12" (30.5 cm)

Patterns:

A10 Body - 1/4"(6 mm) SA; Guidelines for mouth, dart and leg placement; opening between dots, (Join 3 patt ern pieces, matching straight lines at stars)

B10 Upper leg - 1/4"(6 mm) SA; Opening between dots

C10 Lower leg - 1/4"(6 mm) SA; Darts for outer foot;Opening between dots

D10 Mouth - 1/4"(6 mm) SA; Tuck lines for back of mouth

Pieces to cut:

Tie fabrics - 162 of A5 (From Chapter 3)

Interfacing - 162 of B5 (From Chapter 3)

Red lame' - One of D10

Flannel - Two 16"x23"(40.5x 58.5 cm) base pieces

How to make it:

1) Follow the Hexagon Honeycomb basics in Chapter 3 to stabilize the hexagons with interfacing and press under the SA's.

2) Cover both flannel base pieces with hexagons. P/B the hexagons to the flannel matching the pressed edges and embellish with machine satin stitching.

Shirley says: *"Lay out the hexagons so the two base pieces are the mirror image of each other and the tie fabrics will match at the seams."*

3) RST, pin the two hexagon pieces together. Lay out the tie-rannasaurus pieces - A10, two B10 and two C10 - on the pinned pieces. Cut them out through both layers so you have left and right pieces. Staystitch the raw edges of all the tie rannasaurus pieces before you begin.

4) Transfer the dart markings to the WS of all the pieces. Transfer leg placement lines to the RS of the body pieces.

5) Make the head darts. Staystitch the mouth opening and slash it down the center. RST, P/B the body pieces together, leaving an opening between dots to stuff.

6) Stitch the tuck in the mouth (D10) by bringing the lines together. RST, insert the mouth into the mouth opening. Match the dots and the tuck to the back of the mouth. Stitch twice, TT&P, clipping the SA's as needed.

7) Stuff the body firmly. Add pellet stuffing for weight and balance if you like. Slip stitch the opening closed.

8) Make the dart in one leg front only. RST, stitch the leg front to the corresponding undarted leg back, leaving an opening between dots to turn. TT&P, clipping the SA's as needed. Stuff the toe area up to the

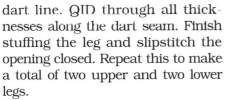

dart line. QID through all thicknesses along the dart seam. Finish stuffing the leg and slipstitch the opening closed. Repeat this to make a total of two upper and two lower legs.

9) Slipstitch the legs to the body at the marks, placing the undarted sides against the body.

Shirley says: "You can attach the legs with buttons as described for Tie-ler the Teddy to make movable joints."

10) Cut two 1"(2.5 cm) circles from the felt. Use pinking shears to shape eyelashes around three-quarters of each circle. Glue the felt eyelashes to the back of each eye and attach the eyes at the marks.Glue pearls around mouth seam.

MY TIE DOLL
Finished size: 13"(35 cm) tall

What you'll need:
Ties - Five in coordinated colors
Muslin - 1/8 yard (0.20 m)
Taffeta - One dark and one light color 1/8 yard (0.20 m) each
Decorative cord 1/8"(3 mm) thick - 1 yards (1.00 m)
Braid trim 1/2"(1.3 cm) wide - 3/8 yard (0.40 m)
Stuffing - 2 ounces (56g)
Pellets - 8 ounces (226g)
Fabric paint - Black, rose & blue
Pink chalk
Blue buttons 3/8"(1 cm) with shank for eyes
Black fringe 4"(10 cm) - 3/8 yard(0.40 m)
Burgundy tassel

Cardboard paper towel tube
Thread for construction and MES
Perfect Pleater

Patterns: (see p.74)
A11 Head - 1/4"(6 mm) SA; Face design lines
B11 Hat - 1/4"(6 mm) SA
C11-Face design

Pieces to cut:
Muslin - Four of A11
Tie for hat - One of B11
Taffeta - Cut one 2" x 28"(5 cm x 71 cm) from the darker color and one 4-1/2" x 28"(11.5 cm x 71 cm) from the lighter color

How to make it:
1) Select two of the ties for the legs. Working on the wider end of the tie, measure 11"(28 cm) up from the point. Draw a line straight across the tie at this point and cut. Trim off the sides of the tie following the edge where it was originally creased so you have a piece about 4"(10 cm) wide. Using this as a pattern, cut a matching piece for the leg back from the rest of the tie. Repeat this to make two pieces for the other leg.
2) Using the narrow end of the tie, cut two arm pieces from each tie as you did for the legs, measuring up 6"(15cm) from the point.
3) RST, P/B the two different leg pieces together at the center front from the neck to the point 5"(12.5cm) below the neck. Repeat to make the back body, reversing the position of the ties. Stitch together and press the seam open.

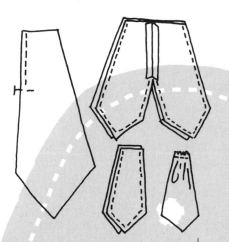

4) RST, P/B the body front and back together around the side and leg edges. Stitch, pivoting at the seam between the legs and leaving the top straight end open. Stitch again just outside the first row of stitches and TT&P. Make two rows of gathering stitches, spaced 1/8" & 1/4"(3 mm & 6 mm) apart around the top opening.

5) RST, P/B two matching arm pieces together. Double stitch around the sides and pointed end. TT&P, then stuff the arm with stuffing and a small amount of pellets. MRE and stitch the top opening closed. Gather the raw edges up as much as possible and knot. Repeat this to make the second arm. Attach the arms to the body at the neck edge.

6) Stuff the legs with stuffing and pellets. Cut a 3-1/2"(9 cm) length of cardboard tube. Pull up the gathers at the neck of the body to fit around the tube. Insert the tube into the opening, stuff the upper body and glue the gathers around the top of the tube. Stuff the tube.

7) RST, stitch two head pieces together at the CF seam of the face. Repeat for the CB seam, leaving a 1-1/2"(3.8 cm) opening to turn. Transfer the face design C11 to the front. Use rose paint for the freckles and nose. Outline the features lightly with black paint. Fill the lips and heart cheeks with rose and the eyes with blue. Rub the pink chalk on scrap paper and then use a cotton swab to blush the cheeks, nose and chin by "scrubbing " the chalk into the fabric.

8) Stitch the front and back of the head together, TT&P. Stuff and slip-stitch the opening closed. Fold the fringe in half, bringing the cut ends to the top edge so they form loopy hair. Glue or stitch them in place. Beginning at the back of the head, glue the hair around the head.

9) RST, stitch the two taffeta strips together along one long edge. Press the SA open and embellish with MES. WST, fold the strip in half matching long raw edges. Crease the fold. Pleat or gather the ruffle to cover the top of the cardboard tube. Turn under the raw edges at the CB, overlap and tack them together. glue the raw edges of the ruffle to the neck area of the head. Cut the cord in half, tie a double bow around the neck and tack it at the CF.

10) Apply glue to the underside neck area of the head. Center over the gathered top end of the body. Pin in place. Allow glue to dry completely.

11) RST, stitch the two straight sides of the hat together. TT&P and tack the tassel to the pointed end of the hat. Glue the hat to the head so only the loopy hair shows. Glue the braid trim on top of the raw edges of the hat to finish.

GOLF CLUB TIE TOP PERS

Finished size: 15-1/2"(39.5 cm) plus pom-pom

What you'll need: (For one)
Ties - Three in coordinate colors
Flannel - 1/4 yard (0.30 m)
Ribbing - 5" x 7"(12.5 cm x 18 cm)
Extra Wide bias tape - 1-1/2 yards (1.40 m)
Knitting worsted weight yarn - 4 oz.
Thread for construction

Pieces to cut:(see steps 1 and 2)
How to make it:
1) Working on the wider end of the tie, measure 13-1/2"(34.5 cm) up

from the point. Draw a line straight across the tie at this point and cut. Trim off the sides of the tie parallel to the edge where it was originally creased so you have a piece about 5"(12.5 cm) wide. Using this as a pattern, cut two more matching pieces from the other ties. Trim off the tie linings.

2) Using the tie sections as a pattern, cut a flannel lining for each one. Baste the flannel to the WS of each tie section.

3) Press under 1/2"(1.3 cm) at the top point of each section. WST, P/B the three sections together, matching the top diagonal and side edges. Stitch them together, using a 3/8"(1 cm) SA.

4) Beginning at the top, press under 1/4"(6 mm) at the end of the bias tape and bind the diagonal and side edge of one seam. Miter the corner. Cut the tape off at the bottom edge and repeat this on the remaining seams.

5) RST, fold the ribbing into a ring, matching the 7"(18 cm) edges. Stitch using a 1/4"(6 mm) SA. WST, fold the cuff in half matching the raw edges and baste them together.

6) Make two rows of gathering stitches, spaced 1/8" & 1/4"(3 mm & 6 mm) from the bottom raw edges. Gather them in to 9"(23 cm). RST, P/B the raw edge of the cuff to the gathered edge, stretching it to fit as needed. Machine stitch, S/O and TRSO.

7) Cut a 3" x 6"(7.5 cm x 15 cm) piece of heavy cardboard. Wind the yarn around it 125 times, cut one side and tie the center together tightly. Repeat this to make five bundles. Tie the centers of all five bundles together securely and shape the pom-pom into 5"(12.5 cm) ball. Shake the pom-pom, trim with scissors and shake again to check the shaping. Tack the pom-pom to the top of the topper.

SOUVENIR TIE BALL

Finished size: Small - 4"(10cm) Medium - 5"(12.5 cm), Large -6-1/2 "(16.5cm) in diameter

What you'll need:

Tie scraps - Assorted colors to equal 3/8 yard (0.40 m) Lightweight fusible interfacing - 1/4 yard (0.30 m)

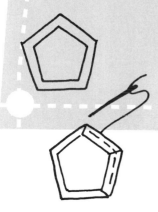
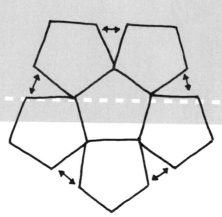

Stuffing - 2 to 4 ounces (28.3 g)
Thread for hand sewing and
    embroidery

Patterns:

A12 Small Pentagon - 1/4"(6 mm)
    SA
B12 Small Stabilizer
C12 Medium Pentagon - 1/4"(6
    mm) SA
D12 Medium Stabilizer
E12 Large Pentagon - 1/4" SA i
F12 Large Stabilizer

Pieces to cut:

Ties - Twelve of the same size for
    each Pentagon ball
Interfacing - Twelve of the corre
    sponding size ball stabilizer

How to make it:

1) Prepare the pentagons following
the Hexagon Honeycomb basics in
Chapter 3 to stabilize the hexagons
with interfacing and press under
the SA's.
2) Slipstitch one side of five different
pentagons to the sides of one center
pentagon. Repeat this to make a
second half.
3) Shaping the pentagons into a
ball shape, match the adjacent
sides of the pentagons and slipstitch them together. Repeat this on
the second half.
4) Place the two halves together,
placing the points of one side into
the indentations of the other.
Slipstitch them together as before,
leaving an opening to stuff. Stuff
and slipstitch the opening closed.
5) To embellish, add a simple hand
embroidery stitch such as the
herringbone worked directly over
the seam of the pentagons.

Shirley says: "Make the small size
into a wonderful Christmas ornament by tucking a ribbon loop inside
before closing up the ball. Then add
a tiny bow at the base of the loop."

🎀 FAMILY TIES ALBUM

Finished size: 11-1/2" x 13"(29 cm
x 33) or smaller

What you'll need:

Tie fabrics - Assorted colors to
    equal 1/4 yard (0.30 m)
Red velvet - 1/2 yard (0.50 m)
Red moire - 1/2 yard (0.50 m)
Muslin & Fleece - 1/2 yard
    (0.50 m) each
Braid trim and cord - 1/2 yard
    (0.50) each
Photo album to cover
Posterboard
White craft glue
Thread for construction and MES

Pieces to cut:

Ties - Assorted strips 1-1/2"
    (3.8 cm) wide
Velvet - See Step 1

How to make it:

1) Draw a vertical line on the front
of the photo album 2-1/2"(6.3 cm)
from and parallel to the spine.
Measure from this line around the
spine to the outer edge of the back
cover. Measure the height of the
album. Add 2"(5 cm) to both measurements and cut that size rectangle from the velvet.
2) Measure the front cover of the
photo album from the line to the
outer edge. Add 2"(5 cm) to the
album height and the front measurement. Cut a rectangle that size
from the muslin.
3) P/B the fleece to the muslin.
Follow the Crazy Strips basics in
Chapter 3 for straight strips to
cover the fleece/muslin with diagonal strips. Embellish the seams
with MES.
4) MRE and stitch the pieced front
to the corresponding edge of the velvet. Press the SA's towards the
pieced front.
5) Use a brush to evenly coat the
front of the album with glue. Align
the seam of the cover with the line
on the album front. Center the
cover so an even amount of extra
fabric extends beyond all edges of
the album. Smooth the cover out
evenly. Apply glue to the spine of
the album and wrap the velvet
around to the back. Repeat this to
glue the velvet to the album back.
Allow to dry.
6) Fold the extra fabric at the outer
edges of the album to the inside
and glue it in place. Miter the corners and trim or clip the fabric as
needed to fit around the binding of
the album.
7) Glue the braid trim/cord next to
the seam on the front cover. Wrap

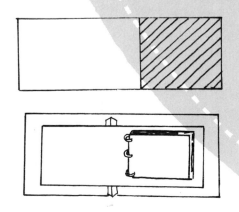

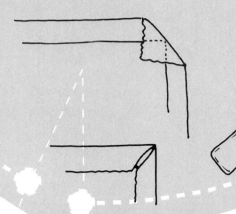

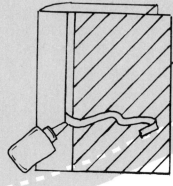

the ends to the inside of the album for 1"(2.5 cm) and glue flat.

8) Measure the size of the front and back inside covers. Subtract 1/2"(1.3 cm) from the measurements and cut two pieces of posterboard to that size. Lay the posterboard pieces on the wrong side of the moire. Cut a piece of moire for each one 1/2"(1.3 cm) larger than the posterboard on all sides. Press the extra fabric over the edge of the posterboard and glue it in place. Miter the corners and clip the fabric so it lays flat. WST, glue the lining pieces to the inside front and back covers.

Shirley says: *"Weight the posterboard down with magazines while drying to prevent curling or warping."*

CHAPTER 6

HOME DEC EFFECTS

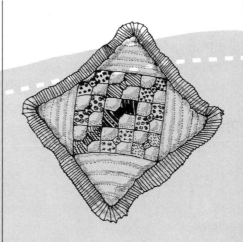

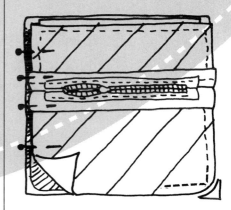 **PILLOW ON POINT**

Finished Size: 16" x 16"(40.5 cm x 40.5 cm) plus ruffle

What you'll need:

Tie fabrics - Nine scraps at least 3" x 8"(7.5 cm x 20.5 cm) each

Taffetas - assorted colors to equal 1/4 yard (0.30 m) at least 3" x 6"(7.5 cm x 15 cm) each

Green velvet - 5/8 yard (0.60 m)

Green taffeta for ruffle - 3/4 yard (0.70 m)

Muslin - 1/2 yard (0.50 m)

Cotton batting - 17" x 17"(43 cm x 43 cm)

Wine piping - 1/2" (1.3 cm) thick 1 - 5/8 yards (1.50m)

Green zipper - 14"(35 cm)

Perfect Pleater tool

Pillow form - 16" x 16"(40.5 cm x 40.5 cm)

Thread for construction and quilting

Patterns: (From Chapter 3)

A3 Bow Tie/Background - 1/4"(6 mm) SA

B3 Bow Tie Knot - 1/4"(6 mm) SA

C3 Base square - 1/4"(6 mm) SA; Bow Tie placement guide lines indicated

Pieces to cut:

Tie fabrics: Two of A3 and one of B3 in the same fabric for each of the nine blocks

Taffetas: Two of A3 in the same color for each of the nine blocks

Green velvet: Two 9" x 16-1/2"(23 cm x 42 cm) pillow backs; Two, 9-1/2" x 9-1/2"(24 cm x 24 cm) squares cut in half diagonally to make four triangular corners

Green taffeta: Five 4-1/2" x 44"(11.5 cm x 112 cm) ruffle strips

Muslin - One 16-1/2" x 16-1/2"(42 cm x 42 cm) backing; Nine of C3

How To Make It:

1) Follow the Bow Tie Basics in Chapter 3 to make nine 4-1/2" x 4-1/2"(11.5 cm x 11.5 cm) blocks.

2) Arrange the Bow Tie blocks in a nine-patch design. Place the "bow ties" so they form diagonal rows across the pillow front.

3) Seam three blocks together into one row. Make three rows. Press the SA's of each row in opposite directions.

4) Seam the rows together, matching the seams where they intersect. Press SA's open.

5) Stitch the long edge of each triangular corner to each side of the patchwork. MRE, layering the batting between the muslin and the patchwork front and P/B. QID on all seams. Quilt five rows in each triangular corner, spaced 1"(2.5 cm)

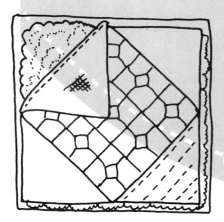

apart, parallel to the seamline.

6) Insert the zipper along the 16-1/2"(42 cm) edges of the pillow backs.

7) Stitch the short ends of the ruffle pieces together into one strip. WST, press the ruffle in half lengthwise. Pleat the ruffle and baste it to the pillow front, easing extra fullness into the corners.

8) RST, P/B the pillow back to the front. Stitch and trim excess fabric from corners. TT&P and insert the pillow form.

🎀 GRANDMA'S TOSS PILLOW

Finished size: 16" x 16"(40.5 cm x 40.5 cm)

What you'll need:

Tie fabrics - Red 3" x 12"(7.5 cm x 30.5 cm); assorted color scraps to equal 1/2 yard (0.50 m)

Red taffeta - 3/8 yard (0.40 m)

Wine velvet - One yard (1.00 m)

Muslin - 3/8 yard (0.40 m)

Cotton batting - 8" x 30 "(20.5 cm x 76 cm)

Wine piping 1/2" (1.3 cm) thick - 1-5/8 yards (1.50 m)

Wine zipper - 14" (35 cm)

Pillow form - 14" x 14"(35.5 cm x 35.5 cm)

Thread for construction and quilting

Patterns: (From Chapter 3)

A1 Grandma's Fan Wedge - 1/4"(6 mm) SA

B1 Grandma's Fan center - 1/4"(6 mm) SA

C1 Grandma's Fan placement guide

Pieces to cut:

Red ties - Four of B1

Assorted tie scraps - Twenty-four of A1

Taffeta - Four 6.-1/2" x 6.-1/2"(16.5 cm x 16.5 cm) squares; four 2-1/2" x 2-1/2" (6.3 cm x 6.3 cm) corners

Velvet - Four 2-1/2" x 22" (6.3 cm x 56cm) borders; two 9-1/2"x16-1/2"(24.5x42 cm) pillow backs

Muslin - FOUR 2-1/2 x1 2-1/2(6.3 cm x 32 cm) border bases

Batting - Four 6-1/2" x 6-1/2"(16.5cm x 16.5 cm) squares

How to make it:

1) Baste the batting squares to the WS of the taffeta squares. Follow the Grandma's Fan basics in Chapter 3 to make four blocks.

2) Arrange the blocks in the pillow front layout. Stitch them into two rows of two blocks each. Join the rows, matching the intersecting seams.

3) Make two rows of gathering stitches, spaced 1/8" and 1/4"(3 mm and 6 mm) apart on all long edges of the four velvet borders. Gather each border to fit one muslin base piece. Adjust the gathers evenly and P/B to the border piece.

4) RST, P/B and stitch one border to two opposite sides of the pillow front. Press SA's towards the borders. Seam one taffeta corner to each short end of the remaining borders. Press the SA's towards the borders. Stitch the border/corner pieces to the pillow front and press as before.

5) Baste piping around the outer edge of the pillow front. Neatly fold the ends back, blend and tack them together where they meet.

6) Insert the zipper along the 16-1/2"(42 cm) edges of the pillow back.

7) RST, P/B the pillow back to the front. Stitch and trim excess fabric from corners. TT&P and insert the pillow form.

 **TIE TABLE RUNNER**

Finished size: 20-1/2" X 54"(52 cm X 138 cm)

What you'll need:

Tie fabric - Sixteen ties in coordinated rusts, greens & browns

Coral background fabric - 1-5/8 yards (1.50 m)

Backing fabric - 1-5/8 (1.50 m)

Cotton batting - 22" x 57"(56 cm x 145 cm)

Thread for construction, quilting and MES

Patterns:(From Chapter 3)

A2 Dresden Plate Wedge - 1/4"(6 mm) SA

B2 Dresden Plate center guide

Pieces to cut:

Ties - From each tie cut three of A2; cut the remaining ties into 3"(7.5 cm) wide bias strips of

various lengths for binding

Background, backing & batting - One 20-1/2" x 54"(52 cm x 138 cm) of each

How to make it:

1) Fold the runner background piece in half lengthwise and crosswise and crease the foldlines with your iron. Measure down from one short end 10"(25.5 cm) and make a mark on both sides of the background. Fold the background at the marks and press to crease. Repeat this at the opposite end of the background. Mark all creaselines with basting.

2) Arrange the sixteen different wedges into the Dresden Plate layout. Follow the Dresden Plate basics in Chapter 3 to stitch the wedges to the background, centering them on the basted lines at the middle of the runner. Repeat this to make a Dresden Plate on each side of the first one, centering them on the basted lines.

3) MRE, layering the batting between the runner and the backing and P/B. Baste the three layers together thoroughly at 4"-6"(10 cm - 15 cm) intervals.

Shirley says: "Use quilter's safety pins to "pin-baste", removing them as you proceed."

4) Embellish the Dresden Plate seams with one MES and use a different MES to finish the inner and outside edges.

5) Outline quilt around each Dresden Plate. To quilt the background, fold the runner into thirds and mark the folds with basting lines. Draw contour quilting lines

around each Dresden plate as follows:

Row 1 - 1/4"(6 mm) outside the Dresden Plate

Row 2 - 1/2"(1.3 cm) out side Row 1

Note: After Row 2, the quilting will not completely circle the Dresden Plate. When the contour quilting meets the basted line dividing the runner into thirds, continue the contour quilting around the next

Dresden Plate.

Row 3 - 3/4"(2 cm) outside Row 2

Row 4 - 1"(2.5 cm) outside Row 3

Row 5 - 1-1/4"(3.2 cm) outside row 4

6) Seam the 3"(7.5 cm) wide bias strips into one continuous 155"(394 cm) length. WST, press the strip in half lengthwise and baste the raw edges together.

7) On the lining side, MRE of the bias strip to the runner. P/B, pressing under the starting end and overlapping to finish. Stitch, pivoting at the corners. Press the binding to the right side, mitering the corners. Slipstitch or machine edgestitch the binding to the front of the runner.

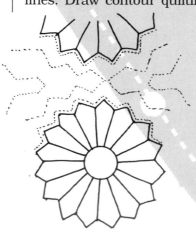

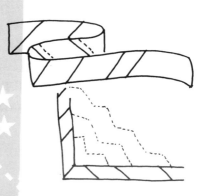

⋈ SHADES OF TIES

Finished size: Any size shade can be used

Note: You are making an opaque shade that light will not pass through.

What you'll need:

Ties - See Step 4
Braid trim to coordinate with ties - See Step 4
Lightweight fleece - See Step 4
Lampshade to cover
Masking tape
White craft glue
Thread for construction and MES

How to make it:

1) Since each shade is different you will need to make your own pattern. Tape pieces of newspaper together to make a sheet large enough for your shade. Tape the straight edge of the newspaper to the seam on the shade. Working on a table, roll the shade so the paper wraps smoothly around the shade. Add more paper if needed. When you reach the seam where you started, trim off the paper evenly with the seam and tape it in place. Next, trim off the excess paper around the edge of the shade at the top and bottom edges. Untape the pattern from the lampshade.

2) Fold the pattern in half. Working on only one half, accurately fold the pattern in half again, then quarters and finally eighths. This divides the shade into sixteen equal sections that will be cut from different ties. This shade section can not be wider than the ties that you have. If necessary, fold the pattern again to get a narrower section.

3) Trace one of the lampshade sections to a separate piece of paper. Add 1/4"(6 mm) SA to both sides of the section and 1"(2.5 cm) to the top and bottom edges. Cut out the pattern with SA's.

4) You will need one tie for each section of the lampshade. Use the large lampshade pattern to estimate the fleece yardage that you need. Measure the circumference of the top and bottom of the lampshade to calculate yardage for the braid trim required.

5) Cut sixteen shade sections from ties using your pattern. Arrange the shade sections into the layout for the shade cover. P/B and stitch them all together. Test fit the cover on the shade. Press the SA's in one direction and embellish the seams with MES if desired.

Shirley says: "If your tie fabrics are flimsy or hard to handle, back the sections with lightweight fusible interfacing before sewing them together."

6) Use the large lampshade pattern to cut out the fleece. Use a brush to evenly coat the shade with glue. Beginning and ending at the seam, position the fleece over the shade. Allow to dry completely.

7) Slip the lampshade cover over the fleece, allowing 1"(2.5 cm) to extend above and below the shade. Pin the cover to the fleece. Fold the extra fabric at the top and bottom of the shade to the inside and glue in place. The shade cover should fit snugly. Clip the fabric as needed so it will lay flat around any wire shade supports.

8) To finish, glue the braid trim over the raw edges on the inside of the shade at the top and bottom.

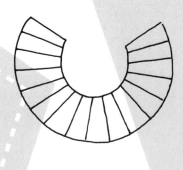

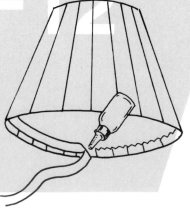

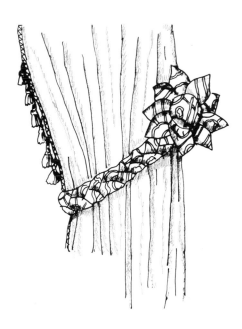

⧓ TERRIFIC TIE-BACKS

Finished size: 29"(73.5) long

What you'll need: (For a pair)

Ties - Six in colors to coordinate with your curtains
Buttons to cover -
   Two 2 3/4"(7 cm)
Plastic rings - Four 1"(2.5 cm)
Posterboard
Thread for construction

Pieces to cut:

Ties - Measure 28"(71 cm) from the narrow end of each tie, mark and cut; From the leftover wide end, cut three 2-3/4" x 5"(7 cm x 12.5 cm) rectangles from each tie; and two 3-3/4" (9.5 cm) circles

Posterboard - Two 3-1/2" (9 cm) circles

How to make it:

1) Select three tie pieces for each tie-back. Tack the finished ends of three together. Use a safety pin and string to anchor the ends to the back of a chair for braiding. Braid the three ties together until you have a tie-back 20"-24"(51 cm - 61 cm) long. Press the raw ends inside the ties and tack them together neatly. Repeat to make a second tie-back with the three remaining ties.

2) RST, fold one of the tie point fabric rectangles in half, bringing the shorter ends together. MRE and stitch one side from the raw edge to the fold. TRSO and press flat positioning the seam in the center of the tie point. MRE and baste them together. Repeat this to make a total of nine tie points for each tie-back.

3) Position the tie points that match the first braided tie-back in a row. With raw edges even, overlap each point to the center of the next one. Put all the seams on the back side. Baste the points together and then gather them up into a ring. Repeat this with the points for the second tie-back.

4) Cover the buttons with leftover tie fabric. Glue the raw edges of one gathered tie point ring to the back of one button. Repeat with the second button.

5) If desired cover the posterboard circles with 4-1/2" (11.5 cm) leftover fabric circles. Press the extra fabric over the edge of the posterboard and glue it in place. Glue the circles to the back of the button rosette, covering the raw edges of the tie points.

6) Tack one plastic ring to each end of both braided tie-backs. Tack the

button rosette to one end of each tie-back, over the ring, so you have a left and right tie-back. Arrange the curtain between the tie-back with the button rosette on the front and hang by a nail with the rings.

⧓ FRAMED AGAIN

Finished size: 3" larger than your photo size

What you'll need:

Assorted ties to equal 1/4 yard (0.30 m)
Coordinating fabric for the frame back and easel cover - 1/4 yard (0.30 m)
Heavy cardboard
Flannel 1/2 yard(0.6m)
Batting
Thick white glue
Large paint brush
Thread for construction

Patterns:

Measure the photo you want to frame. Draw a shape that is 1/8" smaller than the photo. Draw a second shape 3" (7.5 cm) larger on all sides around the first shape. This is

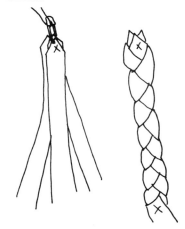

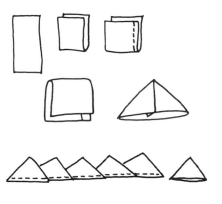

your frame pattern. Transfer these markings to heavy cardboard and cut along the outer marking. Cut out the inside opening of the frame.

Pieces to cut:

Tie scraps - Four 4-1/4" x 4-1/4"(11 cm x 11 cm) corner squares

Batting - Use the frame pattern for the size to cut.

Heavy cardboard - One piece the size of your frame pattern for the frame back; one piece 3"(7.5 cm) wide and 2"(5 cm) shorter than your frame for an easel

Coordinating fabric - Two pieces the size of your frame pattern plus 1/2"(1.3 cm) all around for the frame back; one piece 4"(10 cm) wide and 4"(10 cm) longer than double the length of your easel piece.

How to make it:

1) Follow the Crazy Strips basics in Chapter 3 to make four sections of patchwork for the frame sides. The length of each Crazy Strips section needs to be the length of the inside opening of the frame plus 1/2"(1.3 cm) SA. The width of each Crazy Strips section needs to be 5"(12.5 cm), or the width of your frame plus a 1"(2.5 cm) turn under allowance on the inside and outside edges of the frame.

Shirley says: "The front of the frame can be decorated with any style of patchwork. It looks especially good in the Crazy Chunks technique, as shown on the cover. To make a circle frame, fold the pattern into wedges and piece as you would for the Dresden Plate technique."

2) Lay out your Crazy Strips sections and the corner squares. MRE of the corner squares to the outer raw edge of the Crazy Strips section. Stitch the corner squares to both ends of the top and bottom Crazy Strips sections. Start stitching at the outside edge and stitch to within 1"(2.5 cm) of the inside edge of the Crazy Strips section. Secure thread.

3) Stitch the left and right Crazy Strips sections to the corner squares in the same way to finish the frame front.

4) Apply a thin coat of white glue to the frame with the paint brush. Put the batting on top of this and allow it to dry completely. Trim any excess batting away so it is even with the cardboard around the center opening and outside edges.

5) Put the patchwork down on a table with the wrong side up. Center the frame on top of it, placing the batting against the wrong side of the patchwork. Fold the outer raw edges of the patchwork around to the back of the frame. Do opposite sides first and glue them in place. Miter the corners neatly. Glue the inside edges to the back in the same way.

6) On the frame back, cover one side with fabric, wrapping it around the edges and gluing it flat. Press under 1/2"(1.3 cm) on all raw edges of the remaining fabric piece, clipping and mitering corners as needed. Glue this to the back of the frame, concealing all raw edges. Glue the frame front to the frame back at the top and bottom edges, leaving the sides open to insert the picture.

7) With right sides together, fold the easel cover in half matching the two shorter ends. Stitch the long sides together. TRSO and press. Insert the cardboard easel inside and baste the raw edges closed. Fold the raw edges down and glue them to the back of the frame at the top so it stands up.

NOTE: *You may glue a 4"(10 cm) ribbon stay at the inside bottom edges of the frame and the easel to hold the easel to the frame.*

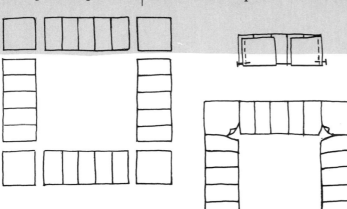

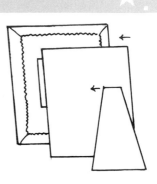

Chapter 7:

CHRISTMAS IS ALWAYS COMING

NO ORDINARY ORNAMENT -
The Lone Star Ornament
Finished size: 4-1/2" x 4-1/2"(11.5 cm x 11.5 cm)

What you'll need:
Tie scraps - Eight colors at least 2" x 6"(5 cm x 15 cm)
Lightweight fusible interfacing - 3/8 yard (0.40 m)
Polyester batting - 4"(10 cm) circle
Decorative cording 1/8"(3 mm) - 3/4 yard (0.70 m)
Thread for construction
White craft glue

Patterns:
A13 Lone Star Diamond - 1/4" (6 mm) SA

B13 Lone Star Diamond Stabilizer

Pieces to cut:
Tie scraps - From each tie scrap cut 2 of A13
Fusible interfacing - Cut sixteen of B13

How to make it:
1) Following the manufacturer's directions, fuse one interfacing diamond to the wrong side of each fabric diamond. Center it on the fabric diamond so 1/4"(6 mm) of fabric is exposed all around.
2) Arrange the eight different diamonds into two matching Lone Star designs that are the mirror image of each other. With right sides together, stitch two adjacent diamonds together. Press the seam open. Repeat this to make a total of four pairs of diamonds. Assemble the mirror-image star in the same way.
3) Stitch two pairs of diamonds together to make a half star. Complete the second half in the same way. Join the halves to make a full star. Press all seams open. Repeat this to make the back of the ornament, leaving a 1-1/2"(3.8 cm) opening in the center seam for stuffing.
4) Baste the 4"(10 cm) circle of batting to the wrong side of the star front. Right sides together, pin and baste the front and back of the star together matching the seams and points. Machine stitch from the back side, leaving a small opening at one indentation of the star for the loop. Machine stitch again just outside the first stitching. Trim the seam allowances and excess batting to 1/8"(3 mm).
5) TRSO and press flat. Use the excess batting scraps to stuff the star. Slipstitch the opening closed.
6) Insert one end of the cord into the opening and secure it with glue. Apply a fine stream of glue to the cord and glue it on top of the star seam around the entire ornament. Cut the end and tuck it into the opening as before. The ends of the cord tend to unravel easily so secure them with tape before cutting. To make a hanging loop, tack the ends of the leftover cord together, tuck them into the opening and secure with glue.

Shirley says: *"To make a tree top star, enlarge the diamond patterns 200%. Assemble the star front and back. Leave the outer star seam open between two points, face the opening with scrap fabric and slip over the top of the tree."*

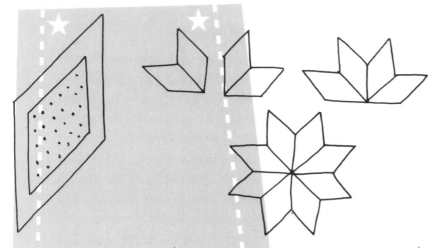

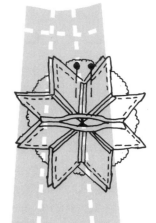

STOCKINGS FOR EVERYBODY

Finished size: 15"(38 cm) tall

What you'll need:

Tie fabrics - Assorted color pieces 1-1/2" x 11"(3.8 cm x 28 cm) or larger to equal 1/4 yard (0.30 m)

Green Taffeta - 3/4 yard (0.70 m)

Taffetas or satins - Assorted color pieces 1-1/2" x 11"(3.8 cm x 28 cm) or larger to equal 1/4 yard (0.30 m)

Muslin - 1/4 yard (0.30 m)

Batting - 18" x 22"(45.5 cm x 56 cm)

Thread for construction and machine embroidery

Patterns:

A14 Stocking 1/4"(6 mm) SA; Mock Cuff Guideline;Strip place ment quideline(Join 2 pattern pieces, matching stars)

Pieces to cut:

Green taffeta - Three of A/B14; one bias grain 4-3/4" x 15-1/2"(12 cm x 39.5 cm) mock cuff; one 2" x 14"(5 cm x 35.5 cm) loop

Muslin & Batting - Two each of A/B14

How to make it:

1) P/B the batting to the muslin so the stocking toe is directed towards the left. Transfer the Mock Cuff Guideline and the strip Guideline to the batting side and mark with a line of basting.

2) Follow the Crazy Strips basics in Chapter 3 to cover the stocking below the Mock Cuff GuideLine with alternating strips of tie fabric and taffetas/satins. Embellish each seam with MES.

Shirley says: "The front of the stocking can be made with any of the techniques in Chapter 3. If you prefer, make a plain stocking and just use the decorative patchwork to add a cuff."

3) P/B batting and muslin to the taffeta stocking back, making sure that you have a mirror image to the front. Mark the mock cuff guideline. RST, stitch the stocking front and back together, leaving the top cuff edge open. TRSO and press.

4) Join the two lining pieces as you did the stocking. WST, insert the lining into the stocking. MRE at the top and P/B.

5) Press 1/2"(1.3 cm) to the WS on each long edge of the loop. WST, fold the loop in half, matching the pressed edges. Edgestitch both sides of the loop. Fold the loop in half, matching the raw ends and P/B them together.

6) RST, stitch the short ends of the bias mock cuff together. Press 1/2"(1.3 cm) to the WS around one edge. RST, match the raw edge of the mock cuff to the guideline around the stocking, placing the seam at the heel side. P/B and stitch 1/4"(6 mm) from the raw edge of the mock cuff. Press the mock cuff up towards the top of the stocking.

7) Fold the mock cuff over the top edge of the stocking. P/B the pressed edge over the seamline on the inside of the stocking. On the heel side, tuck the raw ends of the loop under the pressed edge. Press the loop up to the top of the stocking and tack it to the edge of the mock cuff.

8) Working from the RS, embellish the mock cuff seam with MES.

Shirley says: "This is a medium-size stocking To make a large one, enlarge the pattern 140%. For a small, reduce it to 65%. You can even make adorable stocking ornaments by reducing it by 40%.

Use the techniques in Chapter 3 and your own creativity to make **Stockings For Everybody!** Enlarge or reduce the pattern and decorate the stocking portion or just cuff. The little stocking on the far right uses the narrow ends of nine ties to make a cuff with a jingle bell, decorating each point.

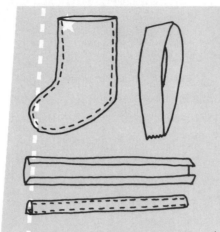

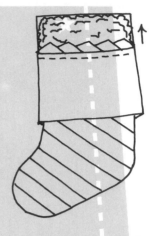

NEXT YEAR'S TREE SKIRT

Finished size: 30"(76 cm) skirt length - 66"(168 cm) diameter

What you'll need:

Whole ties - 48 in assorted reds & burgundy
Lining & Muslin - 4 yards (3.70 m) each
Batting - 70" x 70" (178 cm x 178 cm)
Decorative cording 1/8"(3 mm) thick - 9 yards (8.60 m)
Velcro 1"(2.5 cm) wide - 1/4 yard (0.30 m)
Thread for construction and quilting

Patterns:

A15 Tree Skirt Wedge Bottom
B15 Tree Skirt Wedge Middle
C15 Tree Skirt Wedge Top

Note: *Join 3 pattern pieces, matching stars.*

Pieces to cut:

Ties - 48 of A B C 15
Muslin - Cut the yardage in half crosswise and seam the lengths together along one selvage edge. Cut a 70"(178 cm) circle from the seamed lengths. Cut a 4-1/2"(11.5 cm) diameter tree trunk opening at the center.
Batting - Use the muslin circle as a pattern for cutting.
Lining - Cut and seam the lengths as you did for the muslin. Use the muslin circle as a pattern for cutting; Four 2-1/2" x 2-1/2"(6.3 cm x 6.3 cm) tabs

How to make it:

1) Fold the muslin circle into eighths and press the creaselines. Following any one creaseline, cut from the tree trunk opening to the outer edge to make a back opening. P/B the batting to the muslin and cut it to match and P/B along all the creaselines. Cut the lining so it has a matching opening.

Shirley says: *"Before using the selvage in a project, always trim off the woven edge, or make 1/8"(3 mm) clips, spaced every 3"(7.5 cm). This prevents distortion and shrinkage problems."*

2) Starting at the back opening, baste one tie to the batting. MRE along the back opening and tree trunk opening.
3) RST, MRE of the second tie to the first. S&F it along the seam between the two ties. Press the second tie over and P/B it flat through all thicknesses. Continue adding ties in this manner. Place six ties in each eighth of the tree skirt, using the basted lines as a guide. Trim away the excess batting and muslin around the pointed edge.
4) RST, fold each lining tab in half.

MRE and stitch the long edge and across the short end. TT&P. Cut the Velcro into four equal pieces and separate the two sides. Edgestitch the "hooks" side of each piece to each tab. P/B the raw edges of the tabs to the raw edge of the left back opening, placing one 1/2"(1.3 cm) from the top and bottom edge. Space remaining two tabs about 9"(23 cm) apart between the top and bottom.
5) RST, lay the tree skirt out on the lining circle and P/B the layers together along the back opening and pointed edges. Stitch around all edges of the tree skirt, leaving a 20"(51 cm) opening at one back edge to turn. Trim away the excess lining around the pointed edge, clip as needed and TT&P. Slip stitch the opening closed.
6) P/B the tree skirt layers together along the seams between the ties. QID and make one row of contour quilting in each tie, spaced 1/2"(1.3 cm) from the outer edge of the tie.
7) Match the back opening edges and handstitch the "fuzzy" side of each velcro piece to the lining.
8) Tack the raw end of the cord to the lining at the back opening. Butt the cord against the outer edge of the pointed end of the tie.
Use a narrow machine zig-zag stitch to attach the cording all around the outer pointed edge of the tree skirt, pivoting at the corners. Tack the raw end as before.

Shirley says: *"Use invisible thread (nylon monofilament) to zig-zag the cord in place. It blends with all the different tie colors and is almost undetectable."*

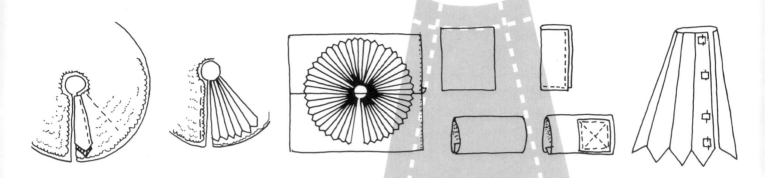

Tie Quickie: Stitch whole ties to a muslin base circle by hand or machine. Begin at the center of the tree skirt and work to the left and right, overlapping the ties at the tree trunk opening as needed. Trim away the excess tie, fold the end to the inside and tack it in place.

BIG BEAUTIFUL WREATH

Finished size: 20"(51 cm) in diameter

What you'll need:

Ties - Assorted reds & greens at least 5-1/2" x 10"(14 cm x 25.5 cm) to equal 3/4 yard (0.70 m)
Green taffeta - 1-1/2 yard (1.40 m)
Batting - 20" x 20"(51 cm x 51 cm)
Stuffing - 16 ounces (453 g)
Thread for construction & MES

Patterns:

A16 Wreath wedge; 1/4" SA

Pieces to cut:

Red ties - Eight of A16
Green ties - Eight of A16
Green taffeta - One 19"(48.5 cm) circle back; 6-1/2"(16.5 cm) wide bias strips to equal 130"(330 cm) for ruffle; 2" x 6"(5 cm x 15 cm) for loop
Batting & Muslin - One 19" (48.5 cm) circle each

How to make it:

1) Fold the muslin circle into quarters and press the creaselines. Open it out and cut a 4"(10 cm) circle in the center. Use this as a pattern to cut the center opening in the wreath back. P/B the batting to the muslin and cut the center opening to match. Mark the creaselines with basting.

2) P/B the first wedge over the batting, so the inner and outer raw edges are even with the muslin and the stitchline is aligned with one of the creaselines.

3) Working clockwise, RST, place the second wedge over the first. Match the raw edges and S&F. Press the wedge over and P/B the raw edges down. Repeat this with the remining wedges, placing four wedges between the creaselines in each quarter of the wreath. Alternate red and green wedges. Slipstitch edge of last wedge in place.

4) Staystitch the inner circle of the wreath front and back, 1/2"(1.3 cm) from the raw edges. Press the SA of both edges to the WS, clipping as needed to make it lay flat.

5) On the outer edge of the wreath front and back, make two rows of gathering stitches, spaced 1/8" & 1/4"(3 mm & 6mm) from the edge. Slightly gather each quarter of the wreath up to 13-1/2"(34.5 cm).

6) Seam the ruffle pieces into a continuous ring. WST, press the ruffle in half lengthwise. Make gathering stitches as before and gather the raw edge to fit the outer edge of the wreath front and P/B.

7) RST, stitch the wreath front and back together around the outer edge. TT&P through the center opening.

8) Match the pressed edges at the center opening. P/B and slipstitch half of the opening together. Stuff the wreath through the opening, slipstitching it completely closed as you proceed.

9) Press all edges of the loop to the WS. WST, fold the loop in half lengthwise, matching all edges. Edgestitch around the loop through all thicknesses. Fold the loop in half and whipstitch it to the CB top edge of the wreath.

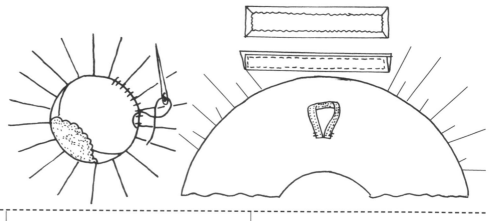

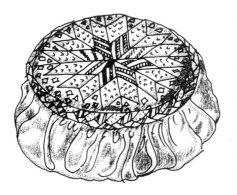

 **WHEN THE BOX IS THE GIFT**

Finished size: 5"(12.5 cm) diameter x 2-1/2"(6.3 cm) high

What you'll need:

Ties - Red to equal 1/8 yard (0.10 m); gold to equal 1/8 yard (0.10 m); blue to equal 1/4 yard (0.20 m)
Bronze taffeta - 1/2 yard (0.20 m)
Lightweight fusible interfacing - 1/4 yard (0.20 m)
Cotton batting - 7" x 7" (18 cm x 18 cm)

Round box to cover 5"(12.5 cm) diameter x 2-1/2"(6.3 cm) high
Posterboard
White craft glue
Thread for construction and quilting

Patterns:

A17 - Lone Star diamond; 1/4"(6 mm) SA
B17 - Lone Star stabilizer

Pieces to cut:

Ties - Eight red of A17; Sixteen gold of A17; Twenty-four blue of A17; One 2" x 20"(5 cm x 51cm) strip of each color
Taffeta - Lid facing 1-3/4" x 18"(4.5 cm x 45.5 cm); Box skirt 4-1/4" x 33"(11 cm x 84 cm);
Box lining 3-3/4" x 16-1/2"(9.5 cm x 42 cm); Three 6"(15 cm) circles
Interfacing - Forty-eight of B17

How to make it:

1) Follow the Lone Star basics in Chapter 3 to assemble the patchwork lid top. Back with batting and

QID.

2) Trace around the box lid on the WS of the quilted star. Add 1/2"(1.3 cm) all around and cut out. Center and glue the star to the box lid. Fold the SA to the side of the lid, clipping if necessary so it lays flat.

3) Press under 1/4"(6 mm) on one long edge and one short end of the lid facing. WST, glue the facing around the lid, covering the SA of the Lone Star. Cover the raw end with the pressed end and glue. Fold the facing to the inside of the lid and glue, clipping as needed to lay flat around the circle.

4) Press the raw edges to the WS on the three 2" x 20"(5 cm x 51 cm) strips. Tack the ends together and braid them, finishing as you started. Glue the braid around the side of the lid, butting the ends and wrapping them with a tie scrap to make them join neatly.

5) RST, MRE and stitch the short ends of the box skirt together. Repeat this on the lining. Make two rows of gathering stitches spaced 1/8"(3 mm) and 1/4"(6 mm) apart around both raw edges. Gather one

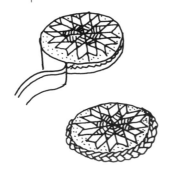

edge to 16"(40 cm). RST, P/B the gathered edge of the skirt to the lining. Stitch and press the SA towards the lining. Slip the box inside so the lining is placed 1/2"(1.3 cm) down from the top of the box edge all around. Working under the skirt, glue the SA to the box. Fold the lining to the inside, clip and glue as you did for the lid.

6) Gather the bottom edge of the skirt to fit 1/2"(1.3 cm) beyond the the box bottom all around. Distribute the gathers evenly and glue them flat to the box bottom.

7) Cut three 4-3/4"(12 cm) circles from the posterboard. Center one posterboard circle on the wrong side of each taffeta circle. Press the excess fabric over the edge, clipping it as needed to lay flat and glue in place. Repeat to cover all the circles. WST, glue one circle inside the lid, one on the inside bottom and one on the outside bottom of the box, covering all the raw edges.

Shirley says: *"Any shape box lid can be covered with ties. Trace the shape on paper and design the patchwork to fit. Use any of the basic techniques in Chapter 3. Use the Crazy Chunk to cover a treasure chest or Grandma's Fan to cover a wedge-shaped box."*

Tie Quickie: *Decorate a finished box with panels of tie fabric or patchwork. Trace the sides of the box you want to decorate onto posterboard. Cut them out and then trim off 1/2"(1.3 cm) on all sides. Cover the posterboard panel with tie fabric and glue it in place on the box. Cover the raw edges with decorative braid trim*

glued around each panel.

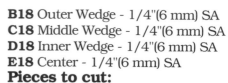 **GRANDMA'S CARD HEART**

Finished size: 8" x 8"(20.5 cm x 20.5 cm)

What you'll need:

Ties - Seven colors at least 3" x 6"(7.5 cm x 15 cm)
Taffeta - 1/4 yard (0.30 m)
Muslin - 1/4 yard (0.30 m)
Batting - 8" x 8"(20.5 cm x 20.5)
Gold cord 1/8"(3 mm) thick - 1-1/2 yard (1.40 m)
Posterboard
White craft glue
Gold bead and tassel
Thread for construction and MES

Patterns:

A18 1/2 Heart Base (Join heart pattern pieces, matching stars) - 1/2"(1.3 cm) SA; Patchwork guidelines

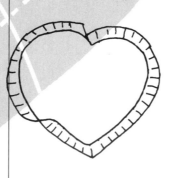

B18 Outer Wedge - 1/4"(6 mm) SA
C18 Middle Wedge - 1/4"(6 mm) SA
D18 Inner Wedge - 1/4"(6 mm) SA
E18 Center - 1/4"(6 mm) SA

Pieces to cut:

Ties - Cut one center (E18) from one color; Use the wedge patterns (B18, C18, D18) to cut a left and right wedge from the remaining six colors
Taffeta - Cut three heart bases (A18)
Muslin & batting - Cut one heart base (A18)

How to make it:

1) P/B the batting to the muslin heart.

2) Beginning at one side, MRE and P/B the outer wedge (B18) to the muslin/batting heart. RST, P/B the middle wedge (C18) on top. Stitch the seam between the two pieces TAT. Press the second wedge over and embellish the seam with MES. Repeat this to stitch all the wedges in place.

3) Make a pressing guide for the center (E18) as described in Chapter 3 - Grandma's Fan. Press under the SA on the curved edge of the center and P/B it to the bottom of the heart so the raw edges of the wedges are covered. Hand applique it in place and embellish the seam with MES.

4) Trim the SA off all edges of the heart base (A18). Cut two hearts from poster board. Trim off an additional 1/8"(3 mm) from the heart base (A18) and cut two lining hearts from the posterboard. Mark these "lining".

5) Center one posterboard heart on the WS of the patchwork heart. Fold the raw edges to the back side, clip-

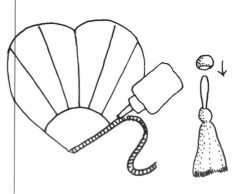

ping them as needed so they lay flat and glue them in place. Repeat this with the taffeta and the second heart. Glue taffeta to the lining hearts in the same way.

Shirley says: *"Use a stiff brush and apply a thin coat of glue to prevent glue from seeping through the fabric. Place a piece of wax paper in between each heart and weight them down with magazines so they dry flat."*

6) Beginning at the bottom point of the patchwork front, glue the end of the cord to the back. Using a fine stream of glue, apply the cording to the entire outer edge of the heart, finishing the end as you did before. Tack the ends of the remaining cord to each side of the heart for the hanging loop, behind the glued cord. Insert the bead onto the tassel loop and tack it to the bottom point.

7) WST, center one lining heart on the back of each outer heart and glue them in place. Glue the front and back of the card heart together, stopping at the point where the hanging cord is attached.

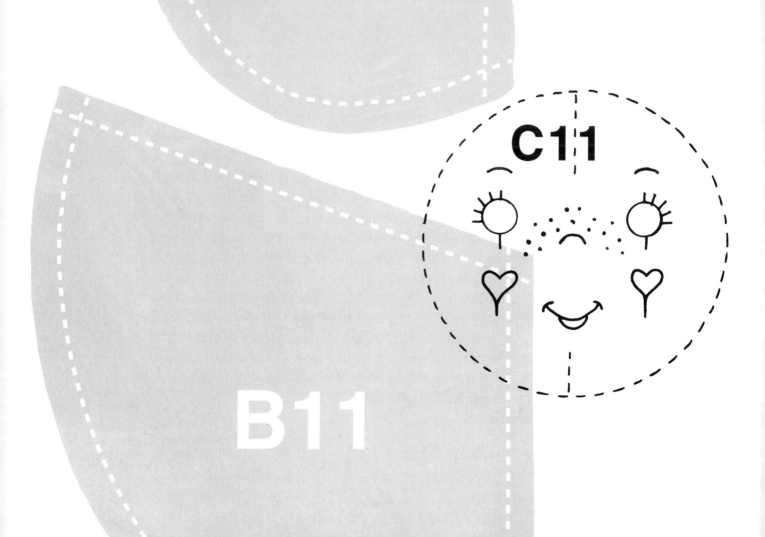

Chapter 8

SMALL QUILTS & WALL QUILTS

🎀 LOG CABIN FEVER

Finished size: 40" x 40"(102 cm x 102 cm)

What you'll need:
One red tie for the center squares
Assorted red ties to equal 3/4 yard (0.7m)
Tie fabrics - Assorted pieces to equal 3/4 yards(0.7m)
Taffeta to coordinate - 3/4 yard (0.70 m)
Flannel-1 yard (1m)
Backing fabric - 1-1/2 yards
Cotton batting - 44" x 44" (112 cm x 112 cm)
Thread for construction and quilting

Patterns: (From Chapter 3) - All pieces include 1/4"(6 mm) SA
A - Center Square
B - Strip 1
C - Strips 2 & 3
D - Strips 4 & 5
E - Strips 6 & 7
F - Strips 8 & 9
G - Strips 10 & 11
H - Strips 12 & 13
I - Strips 14 & 15
J - Strip 16

Pieces to cut:
Red tie - Sixteen of A for center squares
Assorted red ties - Sixteen B, sixteen C, Sixteen D, sixteen E, sixteen F, sixteen G, sixteen H, and sixteen I
Assorted ties - Sixteen C, sixteen D, sixteen E, sixteen F, sixteen G, sixteen H, sixteen I, and sixteen J; 3"(7.5 cm) wide strips of various lengths for the binding
Taffeta - Four 5" x 42"(12.5 cm x 107 cm) border strips
Flannel - Sixteen 8" x 8"(20.5 cm x 20.5 cm) base squares
Backing fabric - Use pieced front for size to cut; one 7" x 37-1/2"(18 cm x 95 cm) for a hanging sleeve
Batting-Use pieced front for size to cut

How to make it:

1) Follow the Log Cabin basics in Chapter 3 to make sixteen Log Cabin blocks.

2) Lay out the Log Cabin blocks in the "Light and Dark" design placing four blocks so the red corners are at the center. Stitch the blocks into four rows. Join the rows.

3) RST, center the border strips on the edges of the quilt top. Stitch to the quilt top, starting and stopping stitching 1/4"(6 mm) from the edges of the quilt top. Miter the corners of the border strips.

4) WST, lay the quilt top on the batting and backing fabric. Baste the layers together and QID around each Log Cabin block. Quilt the border as desired.

5) Seam the 3"(7.5 cm) wide bias strips into one continuous 170"(432 cm) length. WST, press the strip in half lengthwise and baste the raw edges together.

6) On the back, MRE of the bias strip to the wall hanging. P/B, pressing under the starting end and

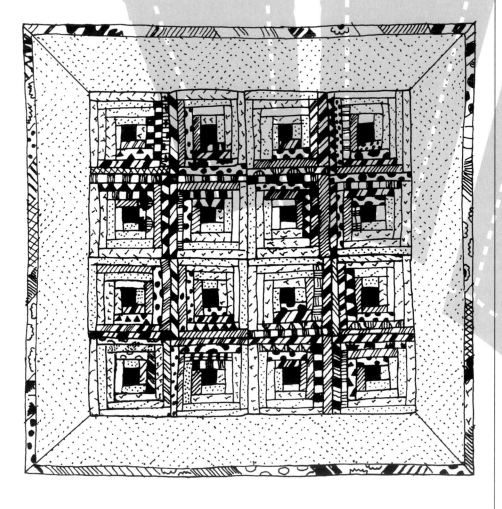

overlapping to finish. Stitch, pivoting at the corners. Press the binding to the right side, mitering the corners. Slipstitch or machine edgestitch the binding to the front of the wall hanging. Make and stich a hanging sleeve to the back side.

Shirley says: *A smaller version of this makes a great pillow, as shown on the cover. Use four 6-1/2" (16.5cm) Log Cabin blocks, using strips A through H. Follow the directions for the Pillow On Point in Chapter 6 to complete the pillow.*

GRANDMA'S FAN FAN TASTIC

Finished size: 49" x 49"(125 cm x 125 cm)

What you'll need:

Red tie for centers to equal 1/8 yard (0.20 m)

Assorted ties to equal 1-1/8 yards (1.10 m)

Bronze taffeta - 1-5/8 yards (1.50 m)

Red taffeta - 5/8 yard (0.60 m)

Backing fabric - 3 yards (2.80 m)

Cotton batting - 54" x 72" (138 cm x 183 cm)

Thread for sewing, quilting and MES

PATTERNS: (From Chapter 3)

A1 - Grandma's Fan Wedge - 1/4"(6 mm) SA

B1 - Grandma's Fan Center - 1/4"(6 mm) SA

C1 - Grandma's Fan Placement guide

D19-Quilting guide

E19-Corner Quilting guide

F19-Border Quilting/Scallop guide

Pieces to cut:

Red ties - Sixteen of B1

Assorted ties - Ninety-six of A1; eighty-eight 2" x 3-1/2"(5 cm x 9 cm) inner border rectangles

Bronze taffeta - Sixteen 6-1/2" x 6-1/2"(16.5 cm x 16.5 cm) background squares; two 5-1/2" x 39-1/2"(14 cm x 100.5 cm) outer border strips; two 5-1/2" x 49-1/2"(14 cm x 126 cm) outer border strips

Red taffeta - Two 17-3/4" x 17-3/4"(45 cm x 45 cm) squares cut in half diagonally for back ground corners; four 3-1/2" x 3-1/2"(9 cm x 9 m) inner border corners

Cotton batting - Sixteen 6-1/2" x 6-1/2"(16.5 cm x 16.5 cm) squares; two 17-3/4" x 17-3/4"(45 cm x 45 cm) squares cut in half diagonally for four back ground corners; four 3-1/2" x 3-1/2"(9 cm x 9 cm) inner corner squares; four 3-1/2" x 33-1/2"(9 cm x 85 cm) inner border strips; two 5 1/2" x 39-1/2"(14 cm x 100.5 cm) outer border strips; two 5-1/2" x 49-1/2"(14 cm x 126 cm) outer border strips

Backing fabric - Use pieced front for size to cut; one 7" x 44-1/2"(18 cm x 113 cm) rectangle for a hanging sleeve

How to make it:

1) Make sixteen Grandma's Fan blocks. MES each block. Quilt a row of scallops at the top edge of the fan and then echo quilt rows to fill the background.

2) Sew four blocks together into one row. Make four rows. Join the rows, matching patchwork and seams where they intersect. Press seams open.

3) Center quilting design D19 to background corners. Baste cotton batting to WS. H/MQ and MES. The decorative stitching simulates the Grandma's Fan design. Make four. Repeat for quilting design E19 on the inner border corners.

4) RST, MRE of long diagonal edge of corner triangles to patchwork center on two opposite edges. Stitch and press seams open. Repeat with remaining corners.

5) Make inner borders by basting the first inner border rectangle, WS, to corresponding cotton batting strips. RST, S&F the next rectangle. Repeat to cover the batting strip. Make four. MES over seams. Stitch an inner border to two opposite sides of the quilt center. Press seams open.

6) RST, stitch one inner border corner to the short ends of the two remaining inner border strips. Press seams open. RST, stitch border/corner units to the quilt center as before. Press seams open.

7) WST, baste outer borders to corresponding cotton batting strips. RST, stitch the outer borders to two opposite sides of the quilt center. Press seams open. RST, stitch remaining outer borders to quilt center. Press seams open.

8) Use outer border quilting design to cut scalloped edge of border. Transfer quilting design to border.

9) Cut backing fabric in half crosswise and seam pieces together at selvage edge. Leave a 20"(51 cm) opening at center to turn. Press

seam open.

10) RST, lay the quilt on top of the backing. Trim backing to fit quilt. P/B and stitch around scalloped edge. TT&P and slipstitch the opening closed.

11) SITD on all construction seams. H/MQ border.

12) Make and stitch hanging sleeve to back side.

BOW TIE BEAUTY

Finished size: 43" x 43"(110 cm x 110 cm) plus tie points

What you'll need:

Assorted tie scraps at least 3-1/2" x 8"(9 cm x 20.5 cm) to equal 2 yards (1.9m)

Assorted taffetas to equal 4 yards (3.70 m)

Black backing - 2 yards (1.90 m)

Muslin for base squares - 5/8 yard (0.60 m)

Cotton batting - 47" x 47" (120 cm x 120 cm)

Thread for sewing, quilting and MES

Patterns: (From Chapter 3)

A3 Bow Tie/Background - 1/4"(6 mm) SA

B3 Bow Tie Knot - 1/4"(6 mm) SA

C3 Base Square - 1/4"(6 mm) SA; Bow Tie placement guide lines indicated.

Pieces to cut:

Tie fabrics - Two of A3 and one of B3 in the same fabric for each of twenty-nine blocks; four 2-1/2" x 2-1/2" (6.3 cm x 6.3 cm) inner corners; twenty-eight 2-1/2" x 6"(6.3 cm x 15 cm) outer border rectangles; forty-two 2-3/4" x 5" (7 cm x 12.5 cm) rectangles for tie points

From assorted taffeta - Twenty-nine pairs of A3; twenty-four 4-1/2"x 4-1/2" squares; thirty-six 2-1/2" x 6"(6.3 cm x 15 cm) outer border rectangles; eight 3 3/4" x 3-3/4"(9.5 cm x 9.5 cm) squares cut in half diagonally for the outer corners; fourty two 2-3/4" x 5"(7 cm x 12.5 cm) rectangles for points

From one color taffeta - Eight 2-1/2" x 6"(6.3 cm x 15 cm) sashing rectangles; four 2-1/2" x 28-1/2"(6.3 cm x 72.5 cm) inner border strips

Black backing - Used pieced front for size to cut backing; one 7" x 42"(18 cm x 107 cm) for hanging sleeve; 1-1/2"(3.8 cm) wide bias strips to equal a length of 185"(470 cm)

Muslin - Twenty-nine of C3 [4-1/2" x 4-1/2"(11.5 cm x 11.5 cm squares)]

Batting - Use pieced front for size to cut

How to make it:

1) Following the Bow Tie Basics in Chapter 3, make twenty-nine 4-1/2" x 4-1/2"(11.5 cm x 11.5 cm) blocks.

2) Follow the layout to seam Bow Tie blocks and taffeta blocks into rows. Press SA open.

3) Stitch one inner border to two

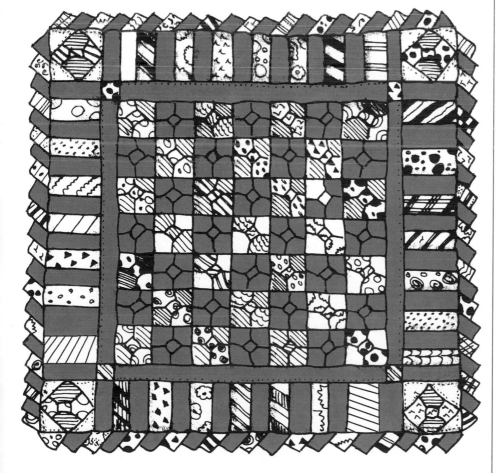

opposite sides of the patchwork. Press SA to border. Seam one inner corner to opposite ends of the remaining inner border strips. Press SA toward border strips. Seam border/corner to remaining edges of patchwork. Press SA to border.

4) Stitch the 2-1/2" x 6"(6.3 cm x 15 cm) rectangles into four strips of fourteen rectangles, alternating the taffeta and tie fabrics, matching the 6"(15 cm) edges. Add a sashing rectangle to each end of the four border strips.

5) Stitch one outer corner triangle to two opposite sides of the patchwork. Press SA toward triangle. Repeat with remaining triangles.

6) Stitch outer borders and corners to patchwork as for inner borders and corners.

7) Layer wall hanging with batting and backing and quilt along all seamlines. To quilt inner border, draw a diagonal line connecting the outer border seam to the center of the blocks, forming squares on point.

8) To make tie points, RST, fold one 2-3/4" x 5"(7 cm x 12.5 cm) rectangle in half, bringing the shorter ends together. MRE and stitch one side from the raw edge to the fold. TRSO and press flat, positioning the seam in the center of the tie points. Make 84. RST, baste twenty-one tie points to each side of the wall hanging.

9) RST, stitch bias strips into one long strip. Press SA's open. WST, press strip in half lengthwise. Stitch bias strip to RS of wall hanging over tie points around outer edges. Press bias away from wall hanging and understitch the seam toward the bias.

10) Press bias strip to the back of the wall hanging. Slipstitch the folded edge of the bias to the back.

11) Make a hanging sleeve and attach to the back of the quilt.

CRAZY CHUNKY HEXAGON

Finished size: 48-1/2"(123 cm) from outer point to outer point

What you'll need:

Assorted tie scraps to equal 1-1/2 yards (1.40 m)
Red taffeta - 1/2 yard (0.50 m)
Purple taffeta - 1/4 yard (0.30 m)
Navy taffeta - 3/4 yard (0.70 m)
Black broadcloth for backing - 1-1/2 yards (1.40 m)
Cotton batting - One 45" x 50"(115 cm x 127 cm) piece; six 14" x 14"(35.5 cm x 35.5 cm) squares
Thread for sewing, quilting and MES

Patterns:

A19 Center triangle
B19 Inner border
C19 Corner
D19 Outer border
Base Triangle To make a pattern piece for the base triangle, draw a line 13"(33 cm) long. Draw a perpendicular line from the center (6-1/2"(16.5 cm) from the end) of the base line, extending up 11"(28 cm). Connect the end of the perpendicular line to both ends of the base line.

Pieces to cut:

Tie fabrics - Six of A19; assorted shape for Crazy Chunks patchwork; 3"(7.5 cm) wide bias strips in various lengths to equal 150"(381 cm) for binding; thirty-six 2-3/4" x 5"(7 cm x 12.5 cm) rectangles for tie points
Red taffeta - Six 2-1/2" x 12-1/2"(6.3 cm x 32 cm) center border strips; six of B19
Purple taffeta - Six of C19
Navy taffeta - Six of D19
Cotton batting - Cut six base triangles;

How to make it:

1) Follow the Crazy Chunks basics in Chapter 3 using the cotton batting base triangles to make six triangles.

2) RST, stitch one triangle A19 to one short end of each 2-1/2" x 12-1/2"(6.3 cm x 32 cm) center border. Start and stop stitching 1/4"(6 mm) from the edges. Press seams open.

3) RST, MRE of center border to one side of a Crazy Chunks triangle. Stitch from the bottom edge to the point, stopping 1/4"(6 mm) from the edge. Alternately stitch three center borders and three tri-

angles together in this manner. Press seams toward center borders.

4) RST, stitch the center triangles together, stopping the stitching where the center/border triangle seams intersect. Press seams open.

5) Make a second half in the same manner.

6) RST, stitch the two halves together. Press as before.

7) RST, alternately stitch corners and inner borders together at the short ends. Start stitching at outer edge and stop 1/4"(6 mm) from inner edge. Press seams open.

8) RST, MRE of inner border to wall hanging. Stitch, matching seams and pivoting at corners as needed. Press seams toward borders.

9) To make tie points, RST, fold one 2-3/4" x 5"(7 cm x 12.5 cm) rectangle in half, bringing the shorter ends together. MRE and stitch one side from the raw edge to the fold. TRSO and press flat, positioning the seam in the center of the tie points. Make thirty-six tie points.

10) Baste six tie points, RST, to the outer edge of each inner border.

11) RST, match short ends of outer borders and stitch as for inner border. Press seams open.

12) RST, MRE of outer border to inner border. Stitch as for inner border, pivoting at corners. Press seams towards inner border.

13) Mark wall hanging for quilting as desired.

14) Use wall hanging for size to cut batting and backing. P/B layers together. Quilt on all seamlines and marked quilting lines.

15) Bind outer edge with bias strips using a 3/4"(2 cm) seam, mitering the corners. Make and stitch hanging sleeve to back side.

LONE STAR STATEMENT

Finished size: 50-1/2" x 50-1/2"(128 cm x 128 cm)

What you'll need:

Red ties to equal 1/4 yard (0.30 m)

Gold ties to equal 1/4 yard (0.30 m)

Mauve ties to equal 3/8 yard (0.40 m)

Blue ties to equal 1/4 yard (0.30 m)

Silver taffeta - 7/8 yard (0.90 m)

Red taffeta - 5/8 yard (0.60 m)

Bronze taffeta - 1/4 yard (0.30 m)

Mauve taffeta - 1/4 yard (0.30 m)

Blue taffeta - 3/4 yard (0.70 m)

Black taffeta - 1 yard (1.00 m)

Black broadcloth for backing - 3 yards(2.75m)

Cotton batting - 53" x 53"(135 cm x 135 cm)

Thread for sewing and quilting

Patterns: (From Chapter 3)

A4 - Lone Star Diamond - 1/4"(6 mm) SA included

B2 -Border quilting guide

Pieces to cut:

Tie fabrics - Eight red (R) A4 for the star center; twenty-four A4 of gold (G); forty A4 of mauve (M); twenty-four A4 of blue (B); eight A4 of red (R) for the star points

Silver taffeta - Four 11-1/2" x 11-1/2"(29 cm x 29 cm) background corners; two 11-7/8" x 11-7/8"(30.5 cm x 30.5 cm) squares cut diagonally to make background triangles; four 2-1/2" x 2-1/2"(6.3 cm x 6.3 cm) inner border corners

Red taffeta (RT) - Sixteen of A4; four 2-1/2" x 37-1/2"(6.3

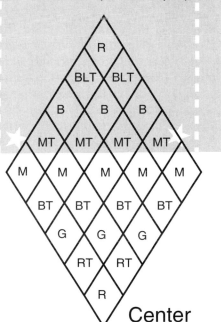

Center

cm x 95 cm) inner border strips; four 5" x 5"(12.5 cm x 12.5 cm) outer border corners

Bronze taffeta (BT) - Thirty-two of A4

Mauve taffeta (MT) - Thirty-two of A4

Blue taffeta (BlT) - Sixteen of A4; four 5" x 41-1/2"(12.5 cm x 106 cm) outer borders

Black taffeta - 3"(7.5) wide bias strips to equal a length of 210"(534 cm)

Black broadcloth -Two 28"x54"(71 cm x 138 cm) backing: one 7" x 49-1/2"(18 cm x 126 cm) rectangle for a hanging sleeve. Use pieced front for size to cut backing

How to make it:

1) Follow the Lone Star basics in Chapter 3 to make the center of the quilt. Set in the background corners and triangles.

2) RST, stitch one inner border to two opposite sides of the quilt top. Stitch one inner corner to the short ends of the two remaining inner borders. Stitch the border/corner strips to the remaining edges of the quilt top.

3) Repeat for the outer borders and corners.

4) Mark the border with the diamond pattern given. Use a diamond grid to mark the background corners and triangles extending the patchwork seams to mark. Channel quilt the inner borders and echo quilt the corner squares.

5) Cut batting and backing to the size of the pieced quilt top.

6) P/B backing, batting and quilt top together TAT. H/MQ all seamlines and marked quilting lines.

7) Bind the outer edges of the quilt. Binding will finish to 3/4" wide.

8) Stitch the hanging sleeve to the back side.

TIES OF A LIFETIME

Finished size: 67-1/2" x 79-1/2"(172 cm x 202 cm)

What you'll need:

Forty-four old ties

Oxford shirting 60"(153 cm) wide - 2-1/8 yard (2.00 m)

Gray flannel - 2-1/8 yard (2.00 m)

Navy blazer fabric - 1/2 yard (0.50 m)

Cotton batting 72"x84"(183x214cm)

Backing fabric -5 yards(4.6m)

Navy bias quilt binding - 9 yards (8.40 m)

Thread for sewing, quilting and MES

Patterns:

A22 - Center tie(Join two pieces, match stars)

B22- Corner tie

C22 - Center oval (one quarter)

D22- Corner center

E22- Center quilting scallop

F22- Corner quilting scallop

Pieces to cut:

Ties (Open ties and remove interfacing, leaving lining in place.) - Forty-four of A22 from the wide end of the tie; forty of B22 from the narrow end of the tie

Oxford shirting - 57-1/2" x 70-1/2"(146 cm x 179 cm) background

Gray flannel - Two 5-1/4" x 57-1/2"(13.5 cm x 146 cm) border strips; two 5-1/4" x 70-1/2"(13.5 cm x 179 cm) border strips

Navy blazer fabric - One C22; one D22; four 5-1/4" x 5-1/4"(13.5 cm x 13.5 cm) corner squares

Backing - Two 37" x 86"(94 cm x 219 cm) rectangles

Batting-use quilt top to cut size

How to make it:

1) Fold background in half crosswise and lengthwise and lightly crease folds. Center pattern C22 over creaseline and trace placement lines for raw edges of ties. Repeat with pattern D22 in each corner.

2) P/B one tie A22 to quilt background, matching seamline to center creaseline. RST, MRE of second tie to first and S&F. Repeat around center oval.Turn under edge of last tie and slip stitch to finish.

3) Repeat step 2 for corners.

4) Slipstitch or MES pointed ends

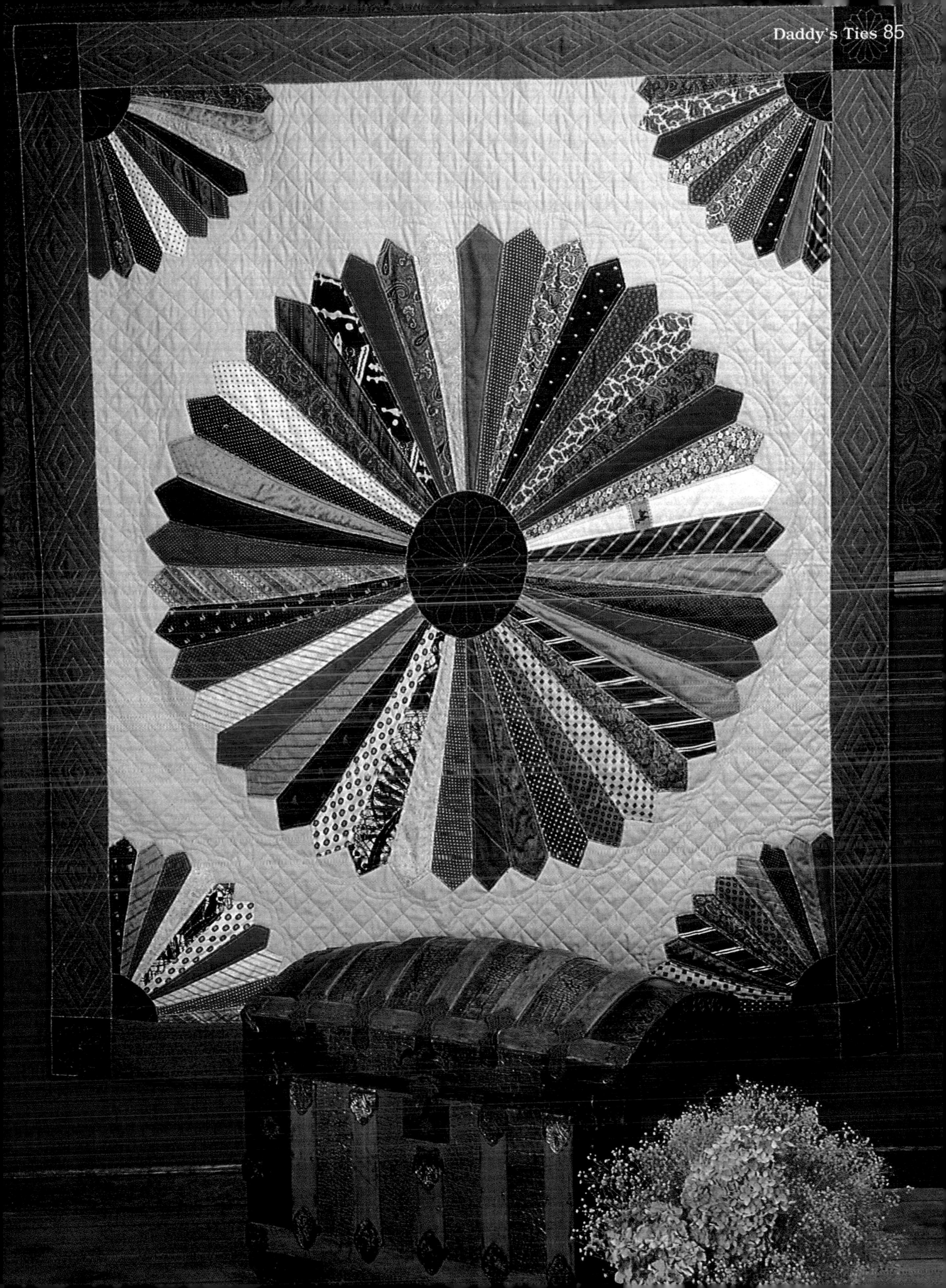

of ties to background. MES seams if desired.

5) Press under curved edges of center pieces C and D. Applique over raw edges of ties.

6) RST, P/B and stitch to two opposite edges of quilt top. Stitch corners to remaining border strips P/B and stitch border/corner strips to remaining edge of quilt top.

7) Mark quilting design on quilt top as desired.

8) Layer backing, batting and quilt top. H/MQ on seamlines and marked quilting lines.

9) Bind edges with quilt binding.

Chapter 9:

ART GARB

ADAPTING YOUR PATTERNS

It's wonderful to hear compliments when I'm wearing one of my own designs. The compliment is usually followed immediately by the question, "Did you make it yourself?" Being able to answer "yes" is not only rewarding but gives me the opportunity to make lots of new friends. It's a great conversation opener and I don't miss a chance to talk about ties and the techniques that I used. Whenever I wear something to a party, I usually end up talking sewing. Now I don't mean that a bunch of women are huddled together in a conference over how to press your seam allowances. Garments made from ties get noticed by everyone. Men are especially interested because when they find out that I've used ties, they like to search the patchwork for a familiar tie fabric that they recognize from their own tie collection. As an

added plus, people get interested in what I'm doing and I've received lots of tie donations from contacts that I would never have met if I hadn't worn my tie garment.

It is impossible to include all the garment patterns here in every size, so I will explain the techniques that I use when I work with commercial patterns. Use these instructions to get started and you will find that soon you're creating your own designs. Keep in mind that these instructions only serve as a guide and will rely on your own resourcefulness. Sewing experience is required. Each pattern is different so it is important to think the process through and make notes on each step. It will be necessary for you to estimate your own yardages, using the commercial pattern as a guide. Excellence in design is frequently based on good problem-solving techniques so don't hesitate to trust yourself and try out your own ideas. The best way to create your own individual look is by learning to adapt commercial patterns to your own original ideas. You can find lots of styles in your size that are easily modified by adding patchwork details and embellishments. When choosing your pattern, always select simple, classic patterns in basic, uncomplicated styles. Avoid those with tucks, pleats, darts and elaborate detailing, seaming or shaping. For your first garment, start with something simple like a vest. After you've got the hang of it, you can move on to more elaborate pieces and then multiple-piece outfits. Thorough planning is the key to success in making a unique garment that you'll be proud to wear for years.

The easiest way to get started is to make a patchwork piece of "fabric" for each pattern section and then just cut the pieces out as if you were using fabric. Make only as much patchwork as necessary to cut out the pattern piece. It is not necessary to make a full rectangle of patchwork. Use the pattern as a guide in assembling only enough to accommodate the garment shape.

It's a good idea to make a patchwork piece slightly larger than each garment pattern section to allow for adjustments. Don't forget to allow for SA's in your planning. Remember to make mirror-image pieces for left and right sections of the garment. Cut the pieces out so they will match along the patchwork seamlines wherever possible. I like to use cotton batting for quilting all my garments. For an extra light quilted effect, split the layers of the batting and use half the thickness. Save all the leftover scraps of patchwork and quilting that are cut away and piece them together later for small projects.

Basic Steps

1) Always make a muslin or a test garment from the pattern you have selected to check the fit and style. Try it on and have a friend help you fit it and get the look just right. Make the alterations to the garment and then check them again.

2) Transfer the exact adjustments and alterations that you made on the test garment to the paper pattern pieces. Always make a duplicate of the pattern to work with and save the original for future projects.

3) Use this adjusted pattern to design your garment. Draw the finished size patchwork blocks or embellishments right on the paper pattern.

4) Pin the pattern together and hold it up in front of a mirror to see how you like it. Change it if necessary. If it just isn't working, start over.

5) Make templates for the patchwork or embellishments based on the design you have decided on. Remember to add seam allowances to all the templates.

6) Estimate the fabrics needed. Always get a little extra just in case.

7) Purchase all the fabrics, notions and trims. Refer to the pattern for a list of materials and yardages.

8) Cut all the patchwork, garment and embellishment pieces.

9) Assemble the patchwork or embellish the garment pieces.

10) Finish the garment following the pattern instructions.

Shirley says: "I have a muslin made up in all my favorite patterns. When I get an idea, I use water-soluble markers to draw directly on the muslin. This way I can try on my idea and refine it before making a pattern and templates. Then I just remove the lines so it's ready when I need it again."

EASY EMBELLISHMENTS

Ties are great for embellishing garments. Update garments that you already have and decorate purchased garments to save time.

Tie tips

Use the tips of ties as you would use prairie points. Insert them into seams and use them for a special edge finish. You can use both the large and the small tips. First, open the back of the tie, remove the interfacing and press the tie out

flat. Leave the lining, facing or hem that finishes the tie tip undisturbed. Measure up 3"(7.5 cm) from the center point and cut straight across the tie so you have a triangle. Repeat this on the narrow end of the tie, making a smaller triangle.

I like to mix up the different colors and sizes of tie tips, overlapping them slightly when inserting them into a seam. To decorate finished seams, line the tie tips up, stitch them to ribbon or trimming and then stitch the ribbon to the garment.

TIE APPLIQUE

Sections of ties are easy to applique on the surface of a garment. First, open the back of the tie, remove the interfacing and press the tie back into it's original shape along the creases. Leave the linings, facings or hems that finish the tie tips undisturbed. Trim off the excess tie fabric from the back so you only have a seam allowance pressed under on each side. Decorate the front of a vest with a grouping of ties, keeping them clear of the armholes and neckline. The bias grain of the fabric allows you some flexibility in placing the ties. Pin one tie down the center of one vest front and then experiment by staggering more ties next to it in different lengths. You can overlap them or butt the edges next each other. Mix colors and patterns and have fun. Try the vest on and see how it's going. Repeat this on the other side. When you like the arrangement, cut the ties off 1"(2.5 cm) beyond the shoulder seam. Press under the raw edges and baste the ties in place. If you have layered several ties, you can trim out the excess fabric underneath to eliminate bulk. If you want to overlap onto the finished edges of the garment, just fold the tie to the inside of the garment and hand stitch it in place. Baste or slipstitch the ties in place. Embroider by hand or machine to secure the ties to the vest. Add quilting, beading or any of your favorite embellishments.

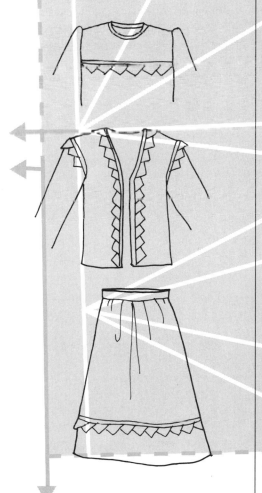

Save all the tie scraps leftover from other projects and use them to create Victorian-style Crazy Quilted details on collars and cuffs. Follow the Crazy Chunk basics in Chapter 3 to cover areas of a garment with scraps. Turn under the SA's so they are finished along the edges of the garment. If possible, you can bind the edges with bias tie strips for a neater finish. This is a great place to show off your hand and ribbon embroidery stitches.

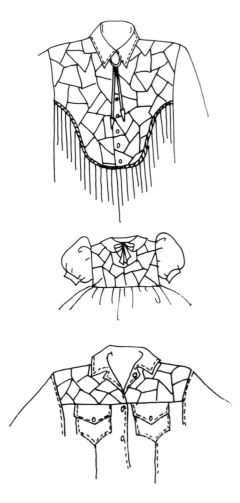

❦ MY FAVORITE VEST

This vest is a good choice for your first garment project. It uses six Grandma's Fan patchwork blocks. Three blocks are placed down the center of each side of the vest front. The remaining area of the vest front is filled in with plain squares in a coordinating color fabric. The plain squares look great when they're filled with quilting in the same design as the patchwork blocks. Use a classic vest pattern and adapt it for the patchwork. Sometimes the point at the bottom of the vest front pattern is too narrow or tapered to accommodate a full patchwork block.

1) Modify the point at the bottom of the vest front so a full block will fit there.

2) Draw a line from the lower point of the vest to the shoulder, parallel to the center front. The patchwork blocks are placed, on point, along this line.

3) Follow the Grandma's Fan basics in Chapter 3 to make six blocks.

4) Make enough plain blocks to accommodate the rest of your pattern. Stitch all the blocks together in diagonal rows and then assemble the rows, placing the fan blocks in the center of each point.

5) Cut the vest front out from the patchwork. If you complete one side first, sometimes you can use portions of the blocks that you trim off to complete the second half. Assemble the opposite side in the same way, so you have a left and right version.

6) Finish the vest following the pattern instructions.

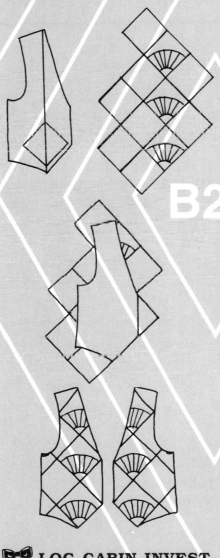

❦ LOG CABIN INVESTMENT

This vest is made just like My Favorite Vest except that you make enough Log Cabin blocks to complete the entire vest front. Draw the blocks out on the vest pattern to determine how many you will need. Follow the Log Cabin basics in Chapter 3 to make 6"(15 cm) blocks. I like to use solid "logs" on half of the block, dividing it diagonally, so it doesn't look too busy. Assemble the blocks for the vest fronts, placing them all in the same direction. Cut out and assemble the vest following the pattern instructions.

❦ SHALL WE CHEVRON?

Follow the Crazy Strips basics in Chapter 3 to decorate the hem section of a princess style jacket that has side front and side back seams. Select a jacket pattern that has eight fairly equal size jacket sections.

1) Cut the jacket pieces out of your jacket fabric. Select the point near the waistline at the CF where you want the chevron to begin. Mark a line at a 45 degree angle to the CF. Arrange the strips so they form a chevron design around the garment.

2) Pin the garment together and try it on and make any adjustments. The basted chevron line should meet at the princess seams. It should form upward peaks at each side front and side back seam.

3) Beginning at the basted line on each section, apply the diagonal strips. Work towards the hemline, covering the jacket bottom completely with strips. End the strips so they match at the at the peaks and valleys of the chevrons. Cut the strips from assorted widths of tie fabric so it is not necessary to match each strip.

4) If you do not want to turn under the raw edges, applique narrow ribbon or trim over the raw edges. If you like, embellish the edges of the strips and ribbons with MES.

5) Fold the sleeve pattern in half lengthwise and cut on the fold. Add a SA to each cut edge. Mark the chevron on the sleeve, measuring up the same amount from the hem point as you did for the jacket. The chevron should form a peak at the seam in the center of the sleeve.

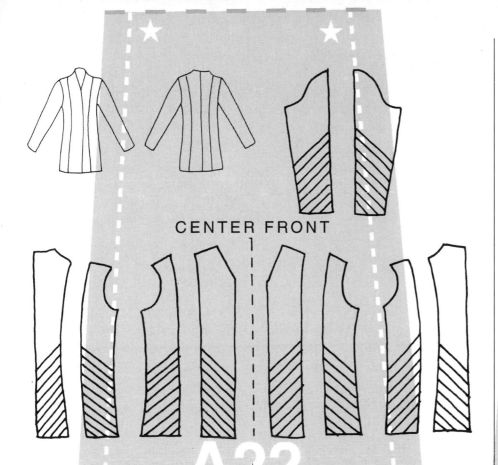

CENTER FRONT

A22

Embellish the sleeve with strips as you did on the jacket. Stitch the two halves of each sleeve together.

6) Back the garment pieces with batting and quilt if you like. Finish the jacket following the pattern instructions.

⬲ SOMETHING REALLY SPECIAL
Advanced level

After you've made a few simple embellished garments, you're ready to move on. Choose a vest or jacket pattern with a plain front that will lend itself to patchwork blocks. Generally it looks best when the seams of the patchwork are parallel to the grainline on the pattern. Follow the Bow Tie basics in Chapter 3 to make 2-1/2"(6.3 cm) patchwork blocks. Reduce the patterns 30%. To determine how many blocks you need, draw a 2-1/2"(6.3 cm) grid over the entire pattern and count the squares. If you're ready for a challenge, plan the patchwork so different colors of spots are formed by the background pieces between the bow ties.

1) First, stitch all the ties and knot pieces to the base squares. Pin them to a piece of tissue paper just as you want them to appear in the garment.

2) Next, pin the backgrounds to the base squares so four of the same color meet at the intersection of the seams between four bow tie blocks. Repeat this with as many colors as you like. Lay out all the blocks for the two fronts on separate pieces of tissue.

3) Working from the pinned layouts, complete the backgrounds for one block at a time and then pin them back in place on the tissue.

4) After all the backgrounds are finished, join the blocks into rows and then assemble the rows into two pieces for the fronts.

5) Cut the vest fronts from the patchwork.

6) If your pattern has a collar, layer and quilt it before assembling the garment. Use commercial templates to plan a decorative quilting design. Or. if you prefer, use a grid or rows of contour and echo quilting.

7) To make pleated edging for the collar, cut a strip of fabric 5"(12.5

cm) wide and about four times as long as the edge where it will be inserted. For a two-color effect, seam a 1-1/2" strip of color A to a 3-1/2"(9 cm) of color B and then embellish the seam with MES. WST, press the strip in half lengthwise. Use the Perfect Pleater to pleat the entire length. Insert the pleated edging as you would a ruffle.

8) Finish the garment following the pattern instructions.

9) For an extra fancy finish, add cording along the outer edge of the fronts and the collar next to the pleating. This can be added using invisible thread and a narrow ZZ, or hand couch the cord in place.

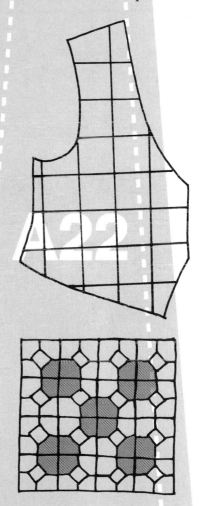

⬲ BOWJOLAIS
Advanced level

This three-piece suit was designed for the 1994 Fairfield Fashion Show. I designed my own patterns and then made the patchwork to fit. You can create a similar

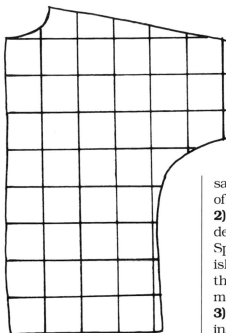

design by adapting your favorite patterns.

Jacket - 2-1/2"(6.3 cm) Bow Tie patchwork blocks
Pattern - Dolman sleeve jacket pattern with plain neckline
Adjustments

1) The jacket is made entirely of 2-1/2"(6.3 cm) Bow Tie blocks like the vest in Something Really Special. Draw a grid on the pattern pieces and count the number of blocks needed. Prepare, make and assemble the blocks as described for the vest.
2) Follow the pattern instructions to finish the jacket. As as alternative finishing idea, bind the edges of the jacket with bias binding in a contrasting color.

Blouse - Chiffon with appliqued spots of tie fabric
Pattern - Plain v-neckline pullover with long full sleeves
Bow Tie Spots A

1) Cut the blouse pieces out from the chiffon. Pin the spots to the garment pieces in a random design, spacing them 2"-3"(5-7.5 cm) apart. Use paper-backed applique fuser to seal the raw edges and secure the spots in place. Work a machine satin stitch around the outer edges of each spot.
2) Make pleated collar and cuffs as described for the Something Really Special vest. The length of the finished cuff pieces should be about three times your wrist measurement.
3) Bind the neckline with contrasting bias. Add a charm at the center.

Skirt - Strip-pieced with quilted appliqued hemline
Pattern - Simple straight skirt with CB zipper

1) Tape the skirt front to the back at the side seam. Using commercial templates, design a quilted border that will be worked around the hemline of the skirt. Work from the CF to the CB and then make a quilted border pattern that will be placed on the CF fold. Add seam allowances and cut the pattern from a solid color.
2) Measure the circumference of the entire skirt. Follow the Crazy Strip basics in Chapter 3 to make a piece of strip piecing to use for the upper section of the skirt.
3) Place the quilted border at the bottom edge of the strip-pieced section. Baste them together. Cut away any excess fabric from underneath the applique. Back the skirt with flannel or cotton batting.
4) Applique the border in place by hand or machine. Quilt the border and strip-piecing.
5) Follow the pattern instructions to assemble the skirt.

🎀 THE ORIGINAL DADDY'S TIES
Advanced level
Dress

Ties - about eighty
Pattern - gown pattern with jewel neckline CB zipper and puffed sleeves and classic vest

1) Measure the length of the dress from the shoulder point to the hem. Add 2"(5 cm) for adjustments. The tie strips are tapered to create a shaped skirt. Make a paper pattern for the tapered strip. Draw a line as long as the dress length. Mark points 3/4"(2 cm) on each side of the line at the top. Mark points 1-1/2"(3.8 cm) on each side at the bottom. Connect the marks with a tapered line. Draw a straight line across the top and bottom ends.
2) Measure the bust circumference of the dress pattern. Divide this measurement by 1"(2.5 cm). This is the number of tapered tie strips that you'll need. Follow the Crazy strip basics in chapter 3 to make strips long enough to cut the tapered pieces.
3) Beginning at the top, stitch the tapered strips together to the waistline point only. From the waistline point down, press under the SA's on each piece. Back the upper section with cotton batting and baste thoroughly.
4) Measure from the waistline to the hem of the pattern and add 2"(5 cm). Make a pattern as you did before for the lace inserts. The width at the bottom is 3"(7.5 cm). Cut one section out to place between each tie strip.
5) Cut the paper pattern front and back off at the waistline. Fold the top assembled dress section in half. Place the front pattern at the foldline and pin. Place the back pattern next to it so the under arm points meet. The patterns will now be positioned as high as possible on top of the pieced bodice sections, ignoring grainlines. The bottom edge of the paper pattern will be used as a placement line for inserting the lace.
6) Insert one lace wedge between each tie strip by placing the point at the waistline at the bottom edge of the paper pattern. Working from the right side, overlap the tie on top

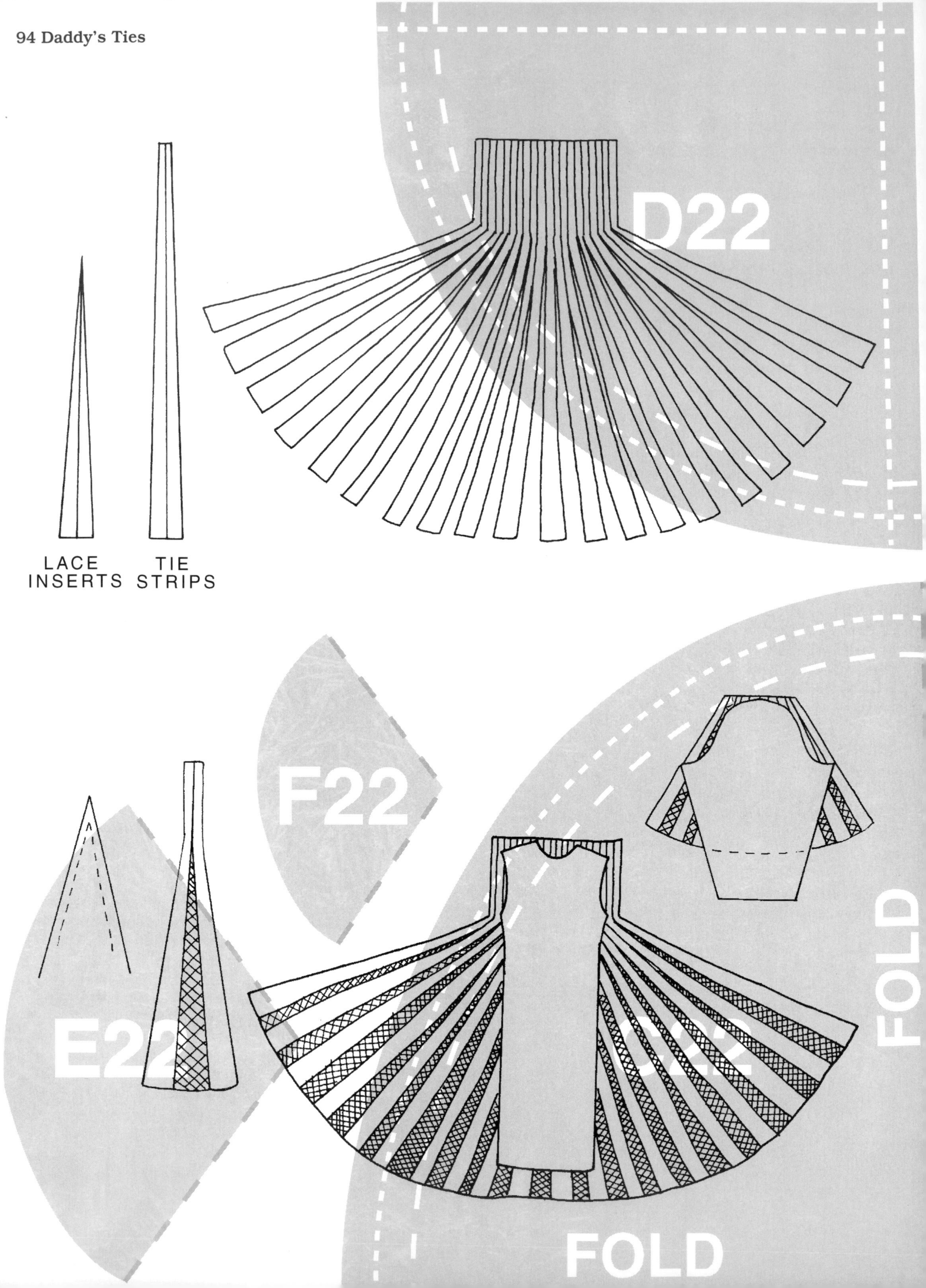

LACE
INSERTS

TIE
STRIPS

D22

F22

E22

C22

FOLD

FOLD

of the lace and ZZ along the pressed edge. At the top of the garment, continue the ZZ between each tie piece.

7) Follow the pattern instructions to assemble the dress. Stitch the CB seam and insert the zipper.

8) Using the sleeve pattern, make 16"(40.5 cm) long lace and tie wedges to accommodate the fullness at the top of the sleeve. Assemble the wedges and finish as you did the dress. Cut the sleeve cap and under arm areas out leaving all the extra fullness remaining at the hem of the sleeve. Gather the cap of the sleeves and insert them following the pattern instructions.

9) Try the dress on and mark even hemlines for the sleeves and skirt. Make a narrow hem finish by hand or machine.

Vest

10) Trim the vest pattern pieces off so they end about 3"(7.5 cm) below the waistline. Follow the Crazy Strip basics in Chapter 3 to make pieces for each garment section.

11) Layer and quilt the sections of the vest. Follow the pattern instructions for assembly.

SOURCE LIST

The list that follows includes only the materials that I have actually used to make the projects in Daddy's Ties. The manufacturers, suppliers and companies named here are only a few of the ones that have wonderful quality products and I am grateful to them for their help. Check the stores in your area for for fabrics, tools and notions. Refer to sewing and craft magazines for the latest information on new products and mail order sources.

TIE SCRAPS

Factory Tie Fabric Scraps - Write for information and availability
    Robert Talbott Studio
    Carmel Valley, CA 93924

    Countess Mara, Inc.
    Toc Drive
    Highland, NY 12528

    W.O. Gamble
    Executive Inn Riverfront

    Paducah, KY 42001

FABRICS

Iridescent Taffeta - Available in most fabric stores and chains
    Rosebar Textiles
    93 Entin Road
    Clifton, NJ 07014

Quilters' Flannel
    Marcus Brothers Textiles,Inc.
    1460 Broadway
    New York, NY 10036

THREADS:

Dual Duty Plus Sewing, Quilting & Metallic Threads
    Coats & Clark Inc.
    30 Patewood Drive
    Greenville, SC 29615

Metallic & Rayon Threads
    Sulky of America
    3113 Broadpoint Drive
    Harbor Heights, FL 33983

TRIMS, TASSELS, CORDS, BRAIDS

    Hollywood Trims
    42005 Cook Street #106
    Palm Desert, CA 92260

BATTING/STUFFING/PILLOW FORMS/PELLETS:

    Fairfield Processing Corp.
    88 Rose Hill Avenue
    Drawer # 1157
    Danbury, CT 06813

BAG SNAP CLOSURES:

Magnetic purse snaps:
    Ghee's
    2620 Centenary
    #3-205
    Shreveport, LA 71104

CHARMS

    Creative Beginnings
    475 Morro Bay
    Morro Bay, CA 93442

FRAMING BOARDS/SUPPLIES:

    Pres-On Merchandising
Corp.
    1020 South Westgate Drive
    Addison, IL 60101

FUSIBLES

Paper-backed and fusible webs
    Heat n Bond
    Therm O Web Inc.
    112 West Carpender
    Wheeling, Il 60090

WASHING LIQUID

    Ensure - Fine Fabric Wash
    The Stearns Technical
Textiles Co.
    100 Williams Street

    Cincinnati, OH 45215

WOOD BOXES:

    Walnut Hollow Farm
    Rt 1
    Dodgeville, WI 53533

TEMPLATES

    Quiltsmith, LTD.
    252 Cedar Road,
    Poquoson,VA
Bow Tie Templates
    Come Quilt With Me
    P.O. Box 021063
    Brooklyn, NY 11202-0023

STENCILS

    The Stencil Co.
    P.O. Box 1218
    Williamsville, NY 14221

INTERFACING

Featherweight lightweight and tricot-fusibles:
    Pellon Corporation
    New York, NY 10018

TOOLS:

The Perfect Pleater - Pleating tool;
Clip-on Tie Knot Maker:
    Clotilde Inc.
    1909 S.W. First Avenue
    Fort Lauderdale, FL
    33315-2100
Rotary Cutters:
    Olfa Products
    Box 747
    Plattsburgh, NY 12901
Rulers:
    Omnigrid
    1560 Port Drive
    Burlington, WA 98233

SEWING MACHINE:

    Bernina of America, Inc
    534 W. Chestnut
    Hinsdale, IL 60521

BIBLIOGRAPHY

Avery, Virginia. Wonderful Wearables. American Quilter's Society, 1991.

Complete Guide to Sewing. Reader's Digest Association, 1976.

Fons, Marianne, and Liz Porter. Quilter's Complete Guide. Oxmoor House, Inc., 1993.

Hatch, Sandra L., and Ann Boyce. Putting on the Glitz. Chilton Book Company, 1991.

Herbort, Diane E. and Susan

Greenhut. The Quiltwear Book. EPM Publications Inc., 1988

The Quilter's Companion: Everything You Need to Know to Make Beautiful Quilts.. That Patchwork Place, 1994.

Lang, Donna and Lucretia Robertson. Decorating with Fabric. Clarkson N. Potter, Inc., 1986.

Poster, Donna. The Quilter's Guide to Rotary Cutting. Chilton, 1991.

Shaeffer, Claire. Fabric Sewing Guide. Chilton Book Company, 1989.

Seward, Linda. Successful Quilting. Rodale Press, 1987.

Wagner, Debra. Teach Yourself Machine Piecing & Quilting. Chilton Book Company, 1992.

Zieman, Nancy. 10-20-30 Minutes to Sew. Oxmoor House, Inc., 1992

INDEX

Thank you for adding **Shirley Botsford's Daddy's Ties** to your library. Every effort has been made to make these instructions clear and accurate. No responsibility is implied for human error, typographical errors or variations in individual workmanship.

For book information:
Chilton Book Company
One Chilton Way
Radnor, PA 19089

As always, I ran out of pages before I ran out of ideas. I have lots more designs for tie projects, plus I'm coming up with new ones everyday. If you're interested in knowing more about ties and what to make with them, just let me know. I'd love to hear from you.

For lecture, workshop and custom designs contact me directly:

Shirley Botsford Designs
P.O. Box 686
Beacon, NY 12508